Praise for
All Things Together

"Heath Hardesty is a pastor whose emerging voice needs to be heard. His setting in the digital Babylon of Silicon Valley, mixed with his unique background as a plumber's apprentice, plus his rare combination of a rapacious mind and joyful, humble demeanor, make him a bright light on the horizon of the American church."

— JOHN MARK COMER, bestselling author of *Practicing the Way*

"It is true, what Iris Murdoch wrote, that perceiving itself is a moral act. Heath has the mind of a sage and the soul of a poet, and he can teach us how to see, so that we will know how to think and feel and live. He is wise in the Way as one who is literate and devout and honest and submitted. I hope this book gains a myriad of readers—and is used to further a glorious movement of apprenticeship to Jesus."

— JOHN ORTBERG, founder of Become New and author of *Steps*

"As conversations about spiritual formation abound, there are dangers and distortions that we are prone to fall into: turning spiritual practices into a curated path to self-optimization or making them an optional add-on, tinkering with one vacuum-sealed area of life we call spirituality. But following Jesus is neither a life hack nor a hobby. Heath Hardesty has painted a vision of the transformed life that doubles as a resistance to those temptations and more. This is discipleship with dirt under our fingernails. This is the formation of the fragments of our lives into a whole image, a mosaic of shards and hues through which the radiance of Christ may pass."

—GLENN PACKIAM, lead pastor at Rockharbor Church and author of *What's a Christian, Anyway?* and *The Resilient Pastor*

"This book is a must-read! Heath's blend of poetic, theological, and helpful makes him one of one. From pastoring to plumbing, this book weaves such beautiful truths in such a compelling way. I'll be buying a boxful to hand out to friends!"

—JEFFERSON BETHKE, *New York Times* bestselling author of *Fighting Shadows*

"Hardesty joins the ranks of Richard Foster and John Stott for spiritual formation for this generation. I'm delighted that this scripturally sound book is birthed here in the Bay Area."

—SHAUNA PILGREEN, author and pastor of Alpha in San Francisco

"Heath interweaves the acquired wisdom of his personal experiences and powerful ideas from other thinkers with the teachings of the biblical authors to showcase the beauty of apprenticeship to Jesus. He does this by practically explaining how Jesus teaches us to become the humans we were designed to be—ones of love, patience, wholeness, and more. Yet Heath also shows his readers that becoming these kinds of people requires us to be with Jesus; and in being with Him, we learn to obey what He says. When we obey what Jesus says, we inevitably become like Him, which is what God always intended for us."

—HAKEEM BRADLEY, biblical scholar,
teacher, blogger, and researcher

"Apprenticeship to Jesus is a beautiful thing to contemplate but an unspeakably difficult thing to live. The path of discipleship is the way of the cross—a road that leads to death. And yet, millions have walked it across the centuries because they've discovered the secret: It is the way to life. It's no small feat to paint an honest vision of the pain of the path with colors so vibrant and true that one can also see its glory. My friend Heath Hardesty has done just that. This book stirred my soul and reminded me why I am committed to the way of Jesus. I believe it will do the same for you."

—JAY Y. KIM, pastor and author

"We have a short time we are given in this world with an urgent entrusted mission to let others know about Jesus. As we share the true gospel and who Jesus is with people, we need to be living out a connected, spiritually healthy life with Him so that our message rings true from our lives. *All Things Together* gives us the ways to be doing that."

—DAN KIMBALL, author of *How (Not) to Read the Bible*
and vice president of Western Seminary

"There are moments where a book takes your pulse, registers that you're on the brink of barely alive, and breathes new life into your lungs. Hardesty's book, *All Things Together,* is water for a thirsty soul. Heath manages to weave personal narrative, poetry, literature, and biblical wisdom into a guidebook for true apprenticeship to our savior. His erudite writing and heartfelt passion shine through, and readers will be enriched and encouraged. Readers, *tolle lege*."

—JONATHAN D. HOLMES, executive director of Fieldstone Counseling and visiting faculty member, CCEF

"With a tone of thoughtfulness and invitation, Heath invites us to lean in and embrace the meaningful life as Jesus-oriented apprentices. Through personal storytelling, references to poetry and literature, and perceptive wisdom laced with conviction and gentleness, Heath shows us the best way forward, the way of apprenticeship to Jesus."

—J. R. BRIGGS, founder of Kairos Partnerships and author of *The Art of Asking Better Questions* and *The Sacred Overlap*

"Heath has a very clear idea here with a unique framework, experience and authority, and a real talent for writing. The large ideas about integration, fragmentation, and the rehumanizing of people in the image of Jesus are just wonderful!"

—JON TYSON, lead pastor of Church of the City New York and bestselling author of *Fighting Shadows*

"Heath's writing offers a unique perspective: a literature major who became an actual apprentice and then a pastor. This background has given him an incredible way with words and powerful insights about the gritty, daily, hands-dirty practice of following Jesus. In this book, Heath offers a road map for embodied discipleship which is relevant and needed in our increasingly digital age."

—NICK CADY, lead pastor of White Fields Community Church in Longmont, Colorado and author of *The God I Won't Believe In: Facing Nine Common Barriers to Embracing Christianity*

"A life following Jesus is often existentially satisfying and unrelentingly ordinary, and in this book, Heath has beautifully presented both. In a contemporary Christian landscape prone to overly mystifying the Christian life, this book calls readers to press into ordinary apprenticeship to Jesus through spiritual disciplines, local church commitment, and time spent with God in the Word and prayer. Perhaps unsurprisingly, it's in these ancient spaces of discipleship that the human heart finds satisfaction to the eternal ache within. Skeptics and saints alike will find much to glean from this book by my dear friend."

—MATT BOGA, associate pastor of Reality Church of Stockton and managing editor for Gospel-Centered Discipleship

"Heath has done something incredibly timely in this moment in redemptive history as people by the millions are being drawn to a life devoted to Christ. He holds out apprenticeship to Jesus as the bull's-eye for the Christian life, and uses a pastor's heart to direct fragmented people like me toward wholeness. Here find a fresh presentation of Christian practices that usher each of us into a fresh encounter with the person of Christ. What a gift."

—BRIAN MCCORMACK, author, speaker, and director of Breakaway at Texas A&M University

"To read *All Things Together* is to encounter Heath Hardesty's voice as many of us know it: openhearted, wise, attentive to Scripture, and deeply attuned to both the beauty and the brokenness of our world. Heath helps us imagine what it means to apprentice ourselves to Jesus in the real world, where distraction, isolation, and dis-integration so often take hold. With thoughtfulness informed by the millennia of the church that predates us, pastoral warmth that is rooted in the present, and a keen eye for the wonder that still pulses through God's world, he offers us a vision of the with-God life that is both inviting and transformative. *All Things Together* will help cast aside the 'wonderblindness' that often clouds our vision. And it must be said: This book is worth reading for the footnotes alone!"

—MIKE NEGLIA, lead pastor at Calvary Cork, Ireland, and host of *Expositors Collective* podcast

"As a former plumber, Heath Hardesty knows a bit about apprenticeship. His book's central claim—that apprenticeship is the essence of Christian life—is thus backed by a refreshing familiarity and authenticity. The result is a beautifully written, practical resource for spiritual formation that will help many readers flesh out their faith. In an age of digital dis-integration, *All Things Together* is a timely apologetic for the truth that brings hope to our hopelessness and cohesion to our chaos: Jesus is Lord."

—BRETT MCCRACKEN, senior editor for the Gospel Coalition and author of *The Wisdom Pyramid: Feeding Your Soul in a Post-Truth World*

All Things Together

All Things Together

How Apprenticeship to Jesus Is the Way of Flourishing in a Fragmented World

Heath Hardesty

Foreword by Jon Tyson

Multnomah

Multnomah

An imprint of the Penguin Random House Christian Publishing Group,
a division of Penguin Random House LLC

1745 Broadway, New York, NY 10019

waterbrookmultnomah.com
penguinrandomhouse.com

A Multnomah Trade Paperback Original

Portions of this work have previously appeared in content owned by Valley Community
Church or are currently used by Valley Community Church for nonsalable purposes.

Trade Paperback ISBN 978-0-593-60262-1
Ebook ISBN 978-0-593-60263-8

The Cataloging-in-Publication Data is on file with the Library of Congress.

Printed in the United States of America on acid-free paper

1st Printing

The authorized representative in the EU for product safety and compliance is
Penguin Random House Ireland, Morrison Chambers, 32 Nassau Street,
Dublin D02 YH68, Ireland. https://eu-contact.penguin.ie

BOOK TEAM: Production editor: Laura K. Wright • Managing editor: Julia Wallace •
Production manager: Kevin Garcia • Copy editors: Lisa Grimenstein, Marissa Earl •
Proofreaders: Darcie Robertson, Rachael Clements

Instagram, X, and Facebook logos: icon - stock.adobe.com

For details on special quantity discounts for bulk purchases, contact
specialmarketscms@penguinrandomhouse.com.

To Marla Joy,
with great love.

Foreword

A Call to an Integrated Life

I've spent most of my life watching people try to follow Jesus while being pulled apart by the forces of our culture. We're a fragmented people living fragmented lives. Our souls are splintered by the ceaseless barrage of information, the relentless ping of notifications, the endless scroll that promises everything and delivers nothing. We've become tourists in our own lives, skimming across the surface of reality without ever diving deep enough to touch bottom. We know more than any previous generation, yet we seem to understand less about what makes for a well-lived life.

That's why Heath's book is such a gift.

He hasn't written another rant against technology or modern life. He has done something far more necessary: He's shown us what it looks like to apprentice ourselves to Jesus in the midst of all this distraction and fragmentation. Not Jesus as a concept or a program, but the living and present Jesus as the living center who holds all things together.

I've noticed over my years as a pastor that we're quite good at compartmentalizing our faith, categorizing it away, while we get on with "real life." We've become experts at knowing about Jesus while remaining novices at living with Jesus. What we need isn't more information, we're drowning in that, but genuine formation into Christ's likeness. We need to learn again what it means to be shaped by the slow, patient, fruit-bearing work of the Spirit in the mess of everyday life.

APPRENTICESHIP TO JESUS

There's something wonderfully concrete about the word *apprenticeship*. It speaks of scars and sweat, of watching and doing, of daily showing up to learn from someone who knows the way. The first disciples weren't mainly known as Christians or believers, they were apprentices, people of the Way, learning to live as Jesus lived by doing what Jesus did. This is what Heath is calling us back to, not a program to complete, not simply new habits to stack, but a whole life to be lived. With all the talk about apprenticeship to Jesus these days, it's refreshing to read from someone who has actually been one in real life, turning wrenches, learning lessons in the trenches, and drawing those lessons deep into an integrated faith through lived experience.

All Things Together works on our imaginations and our practices, teaching us how to:

Live Present in a World of Distraction

I've watched countless people try to squeeze God into the margins of their rushed lives, wondering why their faith feels thin and bloodless. Heath reminds us that presence—real, unhurried attention to God and neighbor—isn't a luxury but the very soil in which the life of faith grows.

Live Formed in a World of Consumption

We've become consumers of spiritual content rather than people being shaped by the living Word. This book calls us back to the patient work of formation, not through quick fixes or three-step solutions, but through the daily practices that shape our loves and reorder our desires.

Live Together in a World of Isolation

The Western myth of the radical individual has infected our spirituality, leaving us trying to follow Jesus alone in a world designed for community. Hardesty recovers the essential truth that we become who we're meant to be only in the company of others who are walking along the same path of becoming whole.

Live on Mission in a World of Cynicism

In an age where words have become cheap and truth claims suspect, we need lives that embody the gospel we proclaim. Not as performance or propaganda, but a faithful presence that is the natural overflow of a life being reshaped by Jesus.

AN INVITATION TO WHOLENESS

But maybe what strikes me most about this book is its rooted-ness. I've seen too many Christians trying to piece together a life of faith from fragments of podcasts, conferences, and social media posts. It doesn't work. We need a center that holds, a way of life that integrates all the scattered pieces of our existence under the lordship of Christ.

Heath isn't offering theories from the safety of abstraction; he's describing a path he's actually walked, complete with the bruises and revelations that come from both plumbing and pastoring, out of the depths of real life. This is what *All Things Together* offers: not a quick fix but a way home. Not inspiration but invitation. Not more spiritual consumption but a path of transformation.

But a word of caution: Don't read this book quickly. Let it read you. Let it expose the places where your life has come unseamed. Let it point you back to the One who takes the scattered fragments and turns them into a flourishing life.

Heath is a pastor and a friend, and in these pages, you will find he becomes a pastor and friend to you too. His vision isn't just that you will read some nice words about the Way, but that the words will lead you to the wonder of the Way Himself, the One in whom all things hold together in love.

Jon Tyson, pastor and author
New York City
Lent 2025

Contents

PART ONE
Re-Imagining
Apprenticeship

For you are great and do wondrous things;
> you alone are God.
Teach me your way, O LORD,
> that I may walk in your truth;
> unite my heart to fear your name.
I give thanks to you, O Lord my God, with
>> my whole heart,
> and I will glorify your name forever.

> —Psalm 86v10–12

What is that which gleams through me, and strikes my heart without hurting it; and I shudder and kindle? I shudder, inasmuch as I am unlike it; I kindle, inasmuch as I am like it.

> —Saint Augustine, *Confessions*

Whoever confesses that Jesus is the Son of God, God abides in him, and he in God. So we have come to know and to believe the love that God has for us. God is love, and whoever abides in love abides in God, and God abides in him. By this is love perfected with us.

> —1 John 4v15–17

1

Blue Collars and Bright Splendors

On Becoming Un-Wonderblind

I am the fool of this story, and no rebel shall hurl me from
my throne.

—G. K. Chesterton, *Orthodoxy*

Earth's crammed with heaven,
And every common bush afire with God,
But only he who sees takes off his shoes;
The rest sit round and pluck blackberries.

—Elizabeth Barrett Browning, *Aurora Leigh*

It is the fall. An uneven V of geese croon their way south
through a bright September sky. A stubborn summer is finally
giving up the ghost as cooler air whispers rumors of snows to
come. You can almost smell the winter storms approaching if
you have lived here long enough. Born here, I can sense the
shifts in the sky and the changes of cadence in the birdsongs.
But in this moment, I am not thinking of the goodness of a
rooted life, one that intimately knows a place and cares to
read its rhythms and decipher its signs. I am not delighting in
the soft bite of the autumn air or the riot of colors spreading
through the locust trees. I am not present to a world "charged

with the grandeur of God."[1] No. I feel like a clenched fist. More Saruman than Wendell Berry.[2]

I don't want to be here.

It is midmorning, and I am in a dingy alley between a collapsing foreclosed home and the old shop fronts of Main Street in the town where I have lived most of my life—Longmont, Colorado. Once known as a cow town on the Front Range, an agricultural community harvesting sugar beets and pumping out metric tons of their bleached sugar, it is now a tech-minded city following the silicon ways of Boulder, its sophisticated neighbor. Here, set against the ancient sentinels of the Rocky Mountains, the towering smokestack of the defunct Great Western Sugar Mill still haunts the skyline—an icon of change and abandoned ways. Its doors closed and its great machines were silenced the year I was born.

A few miles from that long-quiet smokestack, my hands are jammed into heavy leather gloves and my brown Carhartts are smeared dark from the morning's labors. I am lethargic and irritable.[3] Uncomfortable in my skin—cracking my

---

1 Allusions to poetry will abound. This is a line from the brilliant poet-priest Gerard Manley Hopkins. Nods to W. B. Yeats and T. S. Eliot are threaded throughout as well. Also, footnotes don't have to be mind-numbing. I am of the opinion they can be side trails of wonder and extra slants of light for the journey.

2 Saruman is a villainous character in J. R. R. Tolkien's *Lord of the Rings* series. He is a wizard who assists the Dark Lord, and is known for pillaging nature to craft dark machinery. He is described as having "a mind of metal and wheels; and he does not care for growing things, except as far as they serve him for the moment." *The Two Towers*, 2nd ed. (Houghton Mifflin, 1966), 586–87. Wendell Berry, on the other hand, couldn't be further in character from Saruman. He is a novelist, poet, farmer, cultural critic, and environmental activist.

3 Carhartts are a heavy-duty workwear made of durable duck canvas, often worn by construction workers, farmers, and those in the trades.

knuckles and biting my lips. I don't want to be here. I vowed I never would be. So how did I get here?

This is not how my life was supposed to go.

I had zero desire to take up the blue-collared mantle of the family business. Nowhere in my dreams of any desired future were these scenes of turning wrenches or salvaging scrap. Yet here I am, broken pipes in hand and a creeping legion of discontent in my contracted heart. I never set out to work as a service plumber. But now I am spending my days in the dark spaces of homes across town, taking up company with the broken things.

I, I, I—so many *I*'s. This is symptomatic of my problem, but I can't see it. Not yet.

For well over a year, we had been collecting old scrap from our service jobs—cracked copper pipes, battered chrome faucets, broken brass valves, tangles of aluminum, and old leaden waste pipes from turn-of-the-century homes. "One man's trash is another man's treasure" was one of the oft-spoken mottos of blue-collar redemption we lived by. Over time, angular bits and pieces of metal, the unseen guts of old homes, had ended up in our warehouse. The warehouse, just across the alley from the boarded-up home, was in the back of a worn-down 1940s vanilla-brick building that had once been the only bowling alley in town. Now gutted, a few faded bowling pins and lightning strikes remain painted on the structural cinder block walls inside—the concrete still harboring half a century of nicotine. No more glossy wooden lanes, gaudy trophies, or glowing pinball machines.

Sometimes it is hard to imagine how these discarded twistings and long-forgotten fragments were once artfully threaded throughout the walls of new homes, part of a clever network of metal-bound rivers that brought water on demand. These dirty and discarded things were once gleaming channels of life, carrying clean water to draw a bath for a child, fill a pan for Mom's vegetable soup, or water the petunias and Dad's fussed-over heirloom tomato plants. Yet entropy has overtaken them, relentlessly going about its unraveling ways. These pipes were part of ingenious systems all now sadly disassembled, disordered, and distorted. The work of craftsmen now sinking into de-creation. Their integrity could not hold. It is the way of things—to unravel and dissolve, for beautiful order to slouch toward bedlam. Things fall apart. Cheery thoughts, I know. Hang in there.

Today, the master plumber has tasked me to drag out the salvage bins and sort the bits and pieces we have collected. Lead into this pile. Copper and brass over here and there. Slouching and grumbling, I feel rather dragon-like (no epic hoard of gold, though—just these piles of bent metal). I should make it clear: This is not merely a sour mood on a rough Monday. This has become the concave posture of my soul. A collapse. It is the broke-down, ungrateful way I am inhabiting the world. *Incurvatus in se.*[4] I have become a grumble.[5] Combing through the tangled mess of metal, I busy my mind as I keep banging my knuckles about: *How did I get here, sifting through a graveyard of copper bones, pulled from the bodies of countless houses?* Some of the "bones" resurrect a memory of the home from which it came—a floor plan, a

---

4 A Latin theological term most likely coined by Saint Augustine meaning "being curved inward on oneself."

5 In C. S. Lewis's *The Great Divorce,* he paints a portrait of the dehumanizing nature of ingratitude through a grumbler who becomes a grumble.

faucet fixed, a conversation with a homeowner about a book on the shelf or family picture on the wall, or a sudden recollection of where the crawl space and water shutoff valve were located.[6]

I throw a brass shower valve into a pile. Waste. So much waste—and my life feels part of it. To cope, I suppose (or maybe it is sheer pride), I grow philosophical and think: There's something sad about all this. This scrap is the stuff of human ingenuity. This smart technology—temperature-controlled living water at our fingertips within the comfort of our homes—has changed civilizations. Brilliant, really. Almost like magic.

Yet it goes mostly unnoticed and unappreciated, hidden behind the scenes, veiled behind drywall until a toilet backs up or the hot water goes cold. Hidden until we are inconvenienced or we smell our own mortality. We grow so accustomed to good things. Numb to wonders of innovation and savvy design. It's never enough. We take so much for granted. We are wonderblind.

This is my mind urgently searching while my hands are reluctantly working. I suppose I am desperately looking for some meaning, some hidden purpose, some revelatory thought to redeem these seemingly wasted motions, moments, and months. How can I salvage more than these pipes? How can I salvage the fragments of my hopes for how my life would go?

I can feel the resentment in my jaw and teeth. And in the buzzing frustration of it all, there is a profound disconnect between my thoughts and my body. I am a man in pieces.

---

6 I find it strange the things our memory holds on to. Even to this day, I remember in exacting detail countless floor plans and home layouts from service calls.

Riven. Cracked about. Hands and feet, eyes and heart and mind all jumbled and going in different directions as I go about the motions.

In this moment I am unable to feel in my body the importance of my job. There is zero sense of the sacred. No awareness of the glory all around. The comic irony is that I am the one who is wonderblind—unable to see the value of the blue collar I am wearing. Unable to hear the beauty in a dove's call descending from the metal rain gutter above. I am numb to any goodness of the moment. There is not an ounce of mirth in my bones.

And then comes the fire.

Finished with my bleak sorting assignment, I watch the master plumber drag into the alleyway what looks like a small cauldron attached to a blowtorch and a propane tank. On his instruction, we begin throwing the scavenged lead pipes into the heavy cauldron. He turns the noisy burner on. Golden fire flashes. Meditatively, we watch the burning. Without talking, we take in the flame's brilliant dance. Fire has a way of snaring the imagination of little boys and grown men alike.

Slowly, the tangle of dirty metal melts in the thick iron bowl. It merges. It pools. It smooths. My nose wrinkles at the sour smoke, and my eyes squint at the blaring flame—this is certainly not an OSHA-approved activity.[7] But no surprise here, as this master is old school. He plays by different rules from a previous age. Not politically correct in the slightest, he talks about the "old ways." He has plumbing hacks that won't be found in any recent manual. He has stories to tell and retell. He has scars on his hands from slipped wrenches and

---

7 OSHA stands for Occupational Safety and Health Administration.

blowtorched pipes, his marked skin authenticating years of experience. His hands hold scars that say, "I know a better way."

As the heat continues, the wrecked pipes dissolve into a dreary pool, a brown and gray simmering stew. Fire boiling a dull metal-mud under an autumn sky—it all feels a bit primeval. Elemental. Like an ancient recipe for some enchantment. Lines from *Macbeth* come to mind: "Double, double toil and trouble; / Fire burn and caldron bubble. / Fillet of a fenny snake, / In the caldron boil and bake."[8] That, I suppose, is what happens when a literature major becomes a plumber's grumbling apprentice.

Then something happens.

A silver shine flashes out from the bleak bowl. I blink, lean in, and look again. A strange, bright flicker strikes my eyes. The master plumber, unhurried and silent, watching the heat do its severe work, stoops and picks up a heavy iron ladle. He gently dips it into that molten stew, skimming the crusted top and removing the dull dross[9]—the solid impurities freed by the cleansing heat, the waste that was resident in those pipes for untold years. And as he pulls the dross off the top, light is released from beneath the dark crust.

In the crucible sits a radiant looking glass, a brilliant mirror somehow born out of the wreckage of old homes and untold stories. The transformation is staggering. Angular, waste-laden pipes have become an alluring pool of liquid silver, shining with some inner numinous glow. Like Lewis

8 William Shakespeare, *Macbeth,* act 4, scene 1, lines 10–13.

9 Dross is a solid waste product taken off molten metal during smelting. It is unwanted material, and the word is often used to speak of anything that is of low value or quality.

Carroll's wonder-struck Alice, I feel as though I could pass right through the looking glass into some technicolor realm, so clear and full of light as it is. Here in this alley between the broken-down home and the defunct Bowl-O-Rama, some heavenly alchemy has broken in. An alchemy of grace transmuting the mundane moment into something golden.

Is this what hope feels like?

A BRIGHT AND UNEXPECTED IMAGE

That luminous moment was nearly twenty years ago, but what I saw shimmers just as brightly in my imagination today. This is not just a memory. It actively lives within me, for it was not merely something seen, but a reshaping of *how I saw*—a reshaping of my imagination and my way of being.

What could I have seen in a radiant puddle of melted pipes that would be so formative, that would have me tell you of a Monday morning's dreary labors in a filthy alley in Longmont all these years later?

It was not just that some old pipes became a reflective metal pool. That's not it. I understood the chemistry of it. Crucibles do this kind of thing, of course. It was more *personal* somehow, more *intimate*. It was not a science lesson.

It was a soul enchantment, a slant of some deeper magic that had shone through my heart's darkly shaded woods.

As the master plumber stooped to do his strange work, and the dark dross was scooped up and tossed off, there, in the brilliant mirror of that humble crucible, there, in what had been a dismal pool of wreckage, was now a bright and unexpected image. A startling image that would help me see beneath the skin of that moment. An image that would help me see what was happening under the surface of that dingy alley on that cold Monday morning. An image that would help me see what was beginning to gleam underneath the darkened crust of my life.

There, looking up at me from that fire-made mirror, was the clear reflection of the master's image—my father's face. And he was smiling at me.

In that renewed wreckage, I saw my father's delight.

And *that* did it. That fall day my imagination was reshaped in a way I did not and could not comprehend. I could only apprehend the smallest taste, some glimmer of its great importance. Something had happened within me at the sight of that bright and unexpected image of my father's delight backdropped by the sky above.

I suppose that is the case with most soul-reorienting moments—they work like lightning and thunder. The revelation is a swift strike of light, but the meaning comes murmuring across the sky and time at its own unhurried pace. Finally, we hear the voice of what we have seen.

I was mesmerized by the transformation of the forsaken and the forgotten, captivated by the revelation of that mirror and the smiling face it reflected. Awakened by order overcoming entropy. Enchanted by a deep personal goodness, by an abiding delight at the heart of all things. These ideas marked me deeply—would form me—yet it took years to really comprehend their meaning. And being far slower on the uptake than I would like, it has taken me even more time to integrate them, articulate them, and attempt to write about them here in this book. A book that has only a bit to do with plumbing but everything to do with how apprenticeship to Jesus leads to flourishing in a fragmented world.

ABOUT APPRENTICESHIP

This talk of plumbing has much to do with the way of Jesus and the essence of apprenticeship. That bright and unexpected reflection of my father's smiling image spoke of a deep structure of reality, of some foundational principle of the universe. It held flickers of how we humans change. How dragon scales are shed and the beastly and dehumanized take on soft human hearts and skin. How a shadow-person may thicken, may obtain muscle and blood and become more real, more whole, more *truly human.*

The wonder of that bright and unexpected image in a dingy alleyway had much to teach me about the simplicity and complexity of apprenticeship to Jesus—about transformation born of the Master graciously drawing a grumbly soul and bumbling apprentice into the widening goodness and beauty of His life and work.

In that reflection, I saw the universal paradigm of apprenticeship that undergirds all the trades across the world and courses like blood throughout the storyline of Scripture. After all, what is apprenticeship, really? It is important to know that what I am referring to as apprenticeship does not first show up in the Gospels with a blue-collar Messiah, nor in the post-exile rabbinic schools of Israel, nor the schools of ancient Greek philosophy, or even much earlier in the trades—rather, it is baked into the deepest design of the universe.

What I mean by apprenticeship is simply the way human beings—image bearers of God—change. But I am getting ahead of myself. For now, we simply need to know that a paradigm for both apprenticeship in general *and* for apprenticeship to Jesus can be expressed as:

Union → Abiding & Obeying → Imaging

This is the framework or paradigm of apprenticeship at the heart of this book—and at the heart of the way of Jesus.[10] It speaks of the origin (union), the essence (abiding and obeying), and the aim (imaging) of following Jesus. It is a universal, timeless, and time-full paradigm found in all cultures, from the most rural village to the most humming neon city. The truth within this paradigm flows through the arteries of Scripture, Genesis to Revelation, if one has the ears to hear its lub-dubbing pulse.

In the following chapters we will turn through the pages of Scripture and trace the presence of the apprenticeship paradigm along the arc of the biblical drama to see how the origin, essence, and aim of apprenticeship are brilliantly woven in storied form. Then, in part two, we will turn our attention to some vital practices by which apprenticeship to Jesus takes on flesh in our lives. Paradigm, then practices. Imagination, then inhabitation.

My days as a plumber's apprentice have long passed. I have traded my blowtorch and wrenches for my books and my

---

10 Think of a paradigm as "a simple model of a complex reality." I owe this wording to one of my seminary professors, Guy Gray. A paradigm is something like a handheld map that helps you navigate a vast terrain—though small and not exhaustive, it is incredibly formative in someone lost becoming someone found.

study, my leather gloves for counseling sessions and team meetings. Crawl spaces for a pulpit, service calls for hospital visits, weddings, and funerals. I am a pastor now in Silicon Valley of all places—the Oz-like wonderland of Apple, Google, Netflix, Meta, and Tesla. My collar has gone from blue to black, yet my hands still hold the skills and bear the scars from those years of cutting and soldering copper. I can see their ivory lines on my skin as I type.

This move from plumbing to the aches and glad things of pastoring brings me to an often-lost truth in what I will simply call *American Christianity:* that every follower of Jesus is an apprentice. An apprentice graciously called into the family trade, called to observe the Master ply His loving skill, called to abide with Him in familial love, called to trustingly obey what He says, called to intimately know the crucible of transformation that is the way of being formed into His image— called to be a person of love and joy like our good and happy God. Called to integration, to holiness, to be whole, and to revel in the growing harmony of the once-shattered bits and pieces of our humanity. Yet the common absence of apprenticeship Christianity in American churches is a calamity.

Apprenticeship reduced to an option or to spiritual extra credit is a gutting of the gospel. A dis-integration of the essence of the way of Jesus, and a dismantling of the identity of the church. And sadly, it is so terribly common that a call to apprenticeship is often viewed with side-eyed suspicion—like it is some slippery slope into a works-based salvation that denies Jesus as Savior. It has happened countless times over the years—a call to obedience leads to reflexive concerns in the form of "I thought we were a 'grace' people?" or "Won't this lead to some new legalism?" It's a bit like saying, "Marriage? A call to covenant faithfulness? Won't that just lead to adultery and heartbreak?" What a diabolically backward cultural moment.

Apprenticeship to Jesus is not some kind of extra credit for spiritual overachievers added to a standard-level Christianity. It is not an optional way to supersize the basic Christian meal that is dished out in well-branded drive-through-esque services and efficiency-driven programs. *Apprenticeship is the essence of the Christian life.* It is the meat, the *carne,* the *incarnational* substance, the muscle-clad and nerve-entwined body of it all. And the universal essence of apprenticeship is *union* with the Master, which leads to *abiding* with and *obeying* the Master, which then leads to *imaging* the Master. Again:

Union → Abiding & Obeying → Imaging

There is no "Christian" if there is no union with Christ by His Spirit living within us. There is no "Christianity" apart from abiding with Jesus and obeying Him. There is no kingdom of heaven here on earth in which Christians aren't growing, degree by grace-born degree, to image (be like) the King of love and joy.

To be a follower of Jesus is to be an *apprentice* of Jesus. Christianity without apprenticeship to Jesus is a mirage. It's a hollow word. An absurdity. A waterless ocean. It is through apprenticeship to Jesus, a life of *with-ness* with God, that we become like Him, that we become truly human as we practice the way of Jesus in increasing reliance upon His grace. In other words, apprenticeship to Jesus is the way of flourishing—the glorious vocation of being human in which we are made whole and holy. I'll say it again: Apprenticeship to Jesus, at its most basic, is union with Jesus that leads to a life of abiding with and obeying Jesus, which brings about our imaging of Jesus. To be saved is to be saved not only from something but *unto* something. Even more, unto *someone*. When a person undergoes what we call a conversion to the Christian faith, it is an intervening act of God, grace breaking into the gloom and stone of the inward-turned human heart, the bringing about of light and life. It is to be born into a brand-new way of perceiving and inhabiting the world. A whole-life way of being.

PIECES OF THE PROBLEM

Now, there is a problem before us. And it is widening and multiplying, like a crawling crack on a dropped iPhone screen.

We don't see how the pieces and facets of our lives fit into a storied whole.

Our imaginations are fractured and distorted. Our hearts and our narratives are splintered. We are awash in glittering fragments. We pit good things against each other, believing we must choose one over the other. We drift in a sea of cultural debris rising and falling on the tides of our busy days. A jumble of amputated verses, dislocated Bible stories, theological sound bites, tattered threads of traditions, a cargo load of preferences, and maybe a few ancient spiritual practices float about in the prismatic oil slicks of the wreckage. All these bits and pieces knock about, resulting in piecemeal, de-storied, and distorted views of apprenticeship to Jesus, rendering apprenticeship something like a side quest for the more adventure-seeking Christian, but rarely seen as essential to human flourishing.

What we need is a re-storied understanding of the *origin,* the *essence,* and the *aim* of apprenticeship to Jesus, to see how it all fits together in a *with-God life.*[11] We need to re-imagine apprenticeship and to re-inhabit the world in a more holistic way. We need to discover how the cracked and alienated pieces fit, and that it is Jesus who holds all things together.

In a dis-integrated and dehumanized world, most people lack a coherent and integrative narrative about what it means to be human, and more specifically about apprenticeship to Jesus and how it leads to flourishing.

So, please forgive me for any presumption, for my wild-eyed purpose with the pages ahead is aimed at the very reshaping of our imaginations so that we might live in greater accordance with reality. That's all, really—simply reshaping the way we view the world. No big deal, right? I figure it is best to own the audacity of it now. To fish or cut bait, as the saying goes. To go on wildly adventuring toward wholeness, or to close this book and move on to something more *manageable.*

Franz Kafka once said that "a book must be the axe for the frozen sea inside us."[12] I'm no Kafka (which I'm rather glad for). But more than a good cracking of cold seas is needed when it comes to following the way of Jesus. What is even better than an axe to our icy hearts is the warming light of heaven melting the long-frozen waters of the soul. May some warming light come streaming your way if you are in need of it. I am.

So, shall we?

---

11 A marvelous and favorite phrase of Dallas Willard's that I will put to much use.

12 Franz Kafka, *Letters to Friends, Family, and Editors,* trans. Richard and Clara Winston (Schocken, 1977), 16.

2

Imagining Apprentices

An Invitation to See

And as imagination bodies forth
The forms of things unknown, the poet's pen
Turns them to shapes and gives to airy nothing
A local habitation and a name.
—Shakespeare, *A Midsummer Night's Dream*

One will weave the canvas; another will fell a tree by the
light of his ax. Yet another will forge nails, and there will
be others who observe the stars to learn how to navigate.
And yet all will be as one. Building a boat isn't about
weaving canvas, forging nails, or reading the sky. It's about
giving a shared taste for the sea, by the light of which you
will see nothing contradictory but rather a community of
love.

—Antoine de Saint-Exupéry, *Citadelle*

"C'mon. I want to show you something!" He jumped out of
the truck, eyes alight with excitement. He was almost to the
side yard by the time I opened my door and crunched down
onto the gravel driveway of the old farm, too slow for the excitement that pulled him toward the house.

"C'mon! Come and see!" he called back as he led me around

the corner of the house with thin, dilapidated white siding. "*Look!*" he said. And there they were. Peacocks. A half dozen of them swaggering about with no care of us. He walked us toward the closest peacock and whistled and whooped until it stopped and bristled. It considered us for a moment, and then in a flash of light threw open its tail and caught the afternoon sun in the transcendence of trembling turquoise and sapphire feathers. Countless iridescent eyes hovering and blazing, like some otherworldly being had stepped out of the prophet Ezekiel's strange visions.

My father laughed like a child at the lavish display, clapped his hands together in delight, and said, "I'm going to ask Mr. Cobean if I can have some of those feathers! Imagine the beautiful flies I could tie!" He was giddy with the glory of spectral colors and dreams of fly-fishing the St. Vrain river. Milky-eyed, I was wonderblind to the iridescent mystery of it all.

Then we turned and I followed him to the house where we would unclog a laundry sink and he would talk of peacocks and rainbow trout with the widowed homeowner.

Come and see.

This is the call that Jesus extends to two of His soon-to-be apprentices. We read of this alluring encounter in the first chapter of John's gospel, a chapter that is very much about seeing. John is using his words here like flashing lights, calling for our full attention. He wants us to *see* that Jesus is not just to be viewed as an object in our field of sight, but that He is the light by which we view the world.[1] This Jesus is not a mere rabbi who dispenses nuggets of wisdom and tinkers with the

---

1 John 1v4: "In him was life, and the life was the light of men."

shape of our morality; He is the very light by which reality is seen. The light by which we see light.[2] Granted, that might sound strange, but many strange things are quite true.

Somewhere by the muddy banks of the river Jordan, a wild-eyed, rough-hewn prophet with honey on his breath *looks* at Jesus and says, "*Behold,* the Lamb of God." Upon baptizing Jesus, the prophet John (nicknamed "the Baptizer") declares he "*saw* the Spirit" descend from heaven upon Jesus, and that he has "*seen*" and "borne *witness* that this [Jesus] is the Son of God."[3] That's a good bit of seeing in just a few short sentences. We should pay attention.

Witnessing this, and now fascinated, two of John the Baptizer's followers start tailing this intriguing carpenter-now-rabbi named Jesus who "turned and *saw* them following" Him.[4] He sees them. He knows them. He peers into their yawning caverns of need. Jesus skips the shallows and aims for the Mariana Trench of their hearts.[5] He provocatively asks them, "What are you seeking?"[6] What a question! Here is an invitation into the heart of things!

With just a few words Jesus has called them to reassess their existence. What is the churning desire underneath their doings? How do they see the world? Why do they do the things they do? What subterranean longings animate their actions? In turn, they say they want to know where Jesus is stay-

---

2 Psalm 36v9: "For with you is the fountain of life; in your light do we see light."

3 John 1v29–34.

4 John 1v38.

5 The Mariana Trench is the lowest known part of the earth. It plunges to a depth of about thirty-six thousand feet, making it deeper than Mt. Everest is tall.

6 John 1v38.

ing, where He "abides." I wonder, is this a simple curiosity about Jesus's current Airbnb or couch-crashing accommodations, or is this response laden with inklings of the truth that it is only by abiding in Jesus's presence that the soul flourishes?

Regardless of the simplicity or unintentional wisdom of their answer, Jesus calls them to "come and you will *see*."[7] And thus they begin a journey of re-seeing everything. A journey of apprenticeship. Their bodies are called into motion, quickened by Jesus's words. They begin to walk the way of Jesus and learn to see along the journey. In an incredible parallel of the troublesome pattern in Genesis 3 of Eve *seeing* the fruit on the tree of the knowledge of good and evil, *desiring* it, and then *taking* it, here Jesus calls them to *see*, to *desire* God, and to *take up* the good life of following Him.[8] This Jesus-oriented redemptive pattern of seeing, desiring, and taking up will lead to their healing at the true tree of life—the cross of Jesus.

The next bit of narrative draws us further into this theme of seeing.[9] Jesus finds a man named Philip and calls him to follow Him. Philip then does what any good friend would do who encounters something beautiful—he invites his friend to "come and *see*." That is what beauty does. It calls up from within us a deep and ancient reflex to reach out of ourselves to another and invite them to "come and see" that which has dazzled us. This is why two people who are gazing at the same shimmering starfield or molten sunset will utter, "Look at

---

7 John 1v39.

8 One of my professors, Dr. Tim Mackie from BibleProject, introduced me to this reoccurring pattern of seeing, desiring, taking, and eating in one of his brilliant courses at Western Seminary.

9 John 1v43–51.

that!" or "Are you seeing this?" Of course they do! These instinctive words are evidence of how glory makes the soul go centrifugal—outward toward others.

Splendors call us out of isolation and into communion. Beauty is inherently hospitable and generous, stirring us to invite others in. Philip does just that, beckoning Nathanael into something wonderful. John then tells us that Jesus "*saw* Nathanael coming toward him.*" Jesus then enigmatically tells Nathanael, "I *saw* you. . . . I *saw* you under the fig tree. . . . You will *see* greater things. . . . You will *see* heaven opened."[10]

Saw, saw, see, see. Do we see?

Come and see. Become un-wonderblind! Jesus invites us to come and re-see the world the way He sees it. Come and see heaven breaking open on earth, erupting into the middle of the ordinary and familiar. Jesus is after our imaginations. He is after the way we go about our days—how we inhabit the world. He is after every cell, buzzing synapse, and mysterious element that makes up the miracle of our existence.

It turns out that the imagination is not just for some fantasy realm excursion at the movie theater or in the pages of a sci-fi escape. Our imagination is crucial to how we go about the most commonplace activities of our so-called ordinary days. How we grind coffee in the morning. How we answer the day's emails. How we respond to our lonely co-worker. How we hide our anxiety with another glittering distraction or endless to-do list. All these things are very much related to the way we imagine the world to be.

How we imagine our world, how we envision the story in which we live, profoundly shapes the most seemingly insignif-

---

10 John 1v48–51.

icant motions and particularities of our lives. And so, apprenticeship to Jesus has everything to do with our imaginations because apprenticeship to Jesus lays claim to the entirety of our being.

AN EYE LIKE AN OIL LAMP

Jesus really wants us to *see*. He is ever at work teaching in a way that turns our ears into eyes. Using mustard seeds and millstone necklaces, Jesus guides His hearers to re-envision reality. In Jesus's famous Sermon on the Mount, He teaches His listeners about seeing and being. He says, "The eye is the lamp of the body. So, if your eye is healthy, your whole body will be full of light, but if your eye is bad, your whole body will be full of darkness. If then the light in you is darkness, how great is the darkness!"[11]

The eye is the lamp—the light, the guide for how we are to use the body. Just as someone would use an oil lamp in Jesus's day to navigate a dark house, our perception of reality is for navigating this world. In other words, if you don't perceive the world well, you won't live well in the world. If your vision is dark or distorted, your actions won't be aligned with reality, and you will bump about, running into walls and sharp corners, kicking sleeping dogs, and tripping over chairs. But Jesus isn't just talking about our eyes; He is talking about heart problems—how the inner person perceives the world. (Notice He links these thoughts to the human heart and what it treasures just before He talks about the eye being like a lamp.)

---

11 Matthew 6v22–23.

A lamp is for illumination. It is to dispel the darkness and reveal what is there. Jesus wants us to have a healthy way of seeing what is really there. He doesn't want us going around stubbing our toes and headbutting the walls of the universe as we might otherwise do. He uses the word *healthy* (*haplous* in Greek), which means "simple" or "singular."[12] We are to have a "healthy" eye. In other words, we are to see in a way that is not distorted or broken up, but whole, cohesive, and congruent with reality. Jesus wants our sight integrated, not fractured and disorienting. He doesn't want us looking through shattered lenses.

Again, Jesus is not simply asking us to get some proper lenses fit for our eyeballs; He is talking about how we imagine the world. How we apprehend the world in which we live. How all the streams of perceptions and all the bits and pieces come together. Unclear vision leads to confused actions. Planks in our eyes lead to splintered lives. But here is the problem: When we hear the word *imagination,* we are prone to think of something make-believe. Something fabricated. So before we go on, let me share a needed word on the imagination, for it is crucial that we re-imagine apprenticeship to Jesus in a world that has relegated it to an add-on rather than the burning center.

A WORD ON THE IMAGINATION

The imagination is not simply the "fiction faculty" that produces unicorns and orcs; rather, it is the way in which we ap-

---

12 Strong's Greek Lexicon, "haplous," Blue Letter Bible, www.blueletterbible .org/lexicon/g573/kjv/tr/0-1.

prehend the world.[13] This is to say that the imagination is the God-given integrative capacity to see reality. It allows us to apprehend the world, to have a relationship with reality. And, again, how we perceive reality shapes how we live in the world.

Sure, the imagination can generate fiction, can come up with all sorts of wonderful and horrible things—but this is simply one use of it, not its essence. The imagination's primary function is to access reality, to engage what is. To see reality and say, "Yes, now *that* is how things are. *That* is the way of things." The imagination is the faculty of integration, of seeing how all the disparate pieces gather and fit into a vast and unified whole.

Imagination is for reality, and the creation of fiction should always serve what's true. A good sci-fi story should really do something daring to the soul. Dangerous explorations of space should shed light on the black holes and bright horizons of our hearts. *Moby-Dick* should reveal the Ahab-like madness of human pride and the fierce grandeur of an untamable God. Alice's adventures in Wonderland should teach us something about the marvels and dangers of being "curiouser and curiouser." Bluey should induce us to enjoy familial love and value the character formation found in play. A good fairy tale will serve as a training ground for a child to confront evil and loss within a manageable frame. As philoso-

13 *Apprehend* vs. *comprehend:* To apprehend has to do with grasping or perceiving the truth of something intuitively, in a way that is experiential and immediate rather than purely intellectual. To comprehend is to understand something more thoroughly, through reason and systematic analysis. For further discussion of this distinction and for wonderful explorations of a theology of the imagination, enjoy the wise work of the British poet and priest Malcolm Guite. You will thank me later.

pher and neuroscientist Iain McGilchrist wrote, "Imagination is not an impediment, but, on the contrary, a necessity for true knowledge of the world, for true understanding, and for that neglected goal of human life, wisdom."[14]

Fiction helps us see reality to which we are wonderblind. Kisses break curses because being known and loved heals the traumatized soul. Villains appear beautiful because evil is derivative, a plagiarist of the goodness that precedes it and will eternally outlast it. Rings forged by elves are pregnant with power because the artifacts we make have the power to take life, nurture love, and shape cultures. Laboratory-resurrected velociraptors go rogue because there are powers that PhDs and unchecked pride cannot control. Jedis wield lightsabers because, well, they are awesome—and light is the greatest of weapons against the dark side.

The imagination forges fiction to serve reality. But what is the imagination in a more holistic sense? This is the key for us: *The imagination is the integrative faculty by which we apprehend the world; it is how we interface with reality.* It is for this reason that C. S. Lewis wrote, "For me, reason is the natural organ of truth; but imagination is the organ of meaning. Imagination, producing new metaphors or revivifying old, is not the cause of truth, but its condition."[15] This is a crucial point, especially in a world that has mistaken information for wisdom and confused facts for meaning. The meaning of something glows forth from understanding how the pieces

---

14 Iain McGilchrist, *The Matter with Things: Our Brains, Our Delusions, and the Unmaking of the World* (Perspectiva, 2021), 549.

15 C. S. Lewis, "Bluspels and Flalansferes: A Semantic Nightmare," in *Selected Literary Essays,* ed. Walter Hooper (Cambridge University Press, 1969), 157–58.

purposely fit together. Meaning is never found in reduction, only in integration, only in synthesis. The greater explains the lesser. The wonder of the sum explains the parts. So, again, the imagination is not just for fiction, it is the faculty of integration that pulls together the bits and pieces of this world into a meaningful whole. And this includes the integration of our:

- *Affections*—our desires and longings
- *Volitions*—our will and agency
- *Intellections*—our thoughts and memories
- *Emotions*—our psychological states and physiological responses

The imagination is something like a general contractor of the soul who integrates the instrumental work and skills of these many other agents (the subcontractors of affection, volition, intellection, and emotion) in the construction process of a rightly ordered life. A disordered contractor will mismanage good blueprints, misuse valuable resources, pour misaligned foundations, and mislay bricks. Likewise, a misshapen imagination will misapprehend the world, abuse good gifts, inhibit potential, and break things. However, a godly, ordered imagination builds a beautiful life.

In other words, our whole being, *all of us,* is involved in how we see the world. Our thoughts, our will, our desires, our emotions are intertwined. Like rivers, they all flow into the waters of our imagination. For example, why does a young child hide under their covers at night? It is not because they *think* monsters to be a mere fiction. It is because they believe they live in a world where there might really be a monster under the bed or a bogart in the closet.[16] They imagine the world to be a place in which such awful things are quite possible. They have a monster-under-the-bed *plausibility structure*.[17] But it is not just thoughts, not just synapses lighting up in the brain with ones and zeros of data. Scared children hide under the covers because their affections, volitions, intellections, and emotions are caught up in how they imagine the world to be.

Simply put, the child does not desire to be ingested by some toothy monster, and so their body physiologically relates the threat of being devoured with trembling and crying and all senses on high alert (the sympathetic nervous system is humming, and cortisol is pumping!). At the sound in the night that is only the air-conditioning kicking on, adrenaline courses through their little system, and they pull the covers tight, ready to cry out for Mom or Dad or to bravely bolt toward the escape hatch of the bedroom door. This child is inhabiting the world, acting a certain way because of how they imagine the world to be—their entire self is enmeshed and engaged.

Now, it is likely that this child's way of apprehending the world was shaped by something that happened or some story they heard or watched.

Turns out it was my fault.

---

16 A bogart is a creature from the Harry Potter series that takes the shape of your greatest fear.

17 *Plausibility structure* is a term popularized by the Austrian-American sociologist Peter L. Berger. It describes the social conditions and norms that shape what is considered plausible or believable within a society or group.

STORY-FORMED

We recently had a family movie night where there may have been some slightly scary scenes in the adventure tale that growled and glowed from the television. In watching the movie, my way of perceiving the world was being shaped. My way of seeing the world was recharged with wonder— amazed at human creativity and cinematic skill, and enlivened through a resurgence of my childhood desires to swashbuckle evil and seek out hidden treasure. But I was not watching alone. My youngest daughter's way of seeing the world was also being shaped—with a brand-new plausibility structure that included scaly monsters and nefarious black carriages that carry children away into the night.[18] The power of the story worked on her intellect, her will, and her desires, and ignited her emotions. How she was now imagining the world would reflexively translate into how she inhabited it, and its consequences meant a night of far too little sleep for her, for Mom, and for Dad.

Stories hold immense formative power. They don't simply traffic in information, shuttling about and stringing data together. Stories are integrators. Aggregators of significance. Sinews. They assemble the wild pieces of the world into a meaningful whole. They bring form and order to the sound and the fury of raw experience that rushes at us moment by moment. Like a super-magnet, stories pull together the charged fragments of existence, giving us a vision and experi-

---

18 I cannot recommend highly enough the books of *The Wingfeather Saga* by Andrew Peterson. They are loaded with laughter and danger, perfect for helping children (and adults) learn to navigate the world well.

ence of what is or what could be or what should never come about.

Stories lay hold of desires, emotions, the will, and the intellect. That is, stories lay glorious or destructive siege upon the imagination. This is why we remember stories far more than we can recall dislocated data or abstractions. It has often happened that someone will retell a story to me that I told years ago in a sermon, sharing with me how it has shaped them; yet on the very Monday after a sermon, most of the data and abstractions in it have already evaporated like a mist.

We are story-formed beings. Stories sculpt the world we inhabit; they fashion our self-understandings, tether our experiences, and then take on flesh in our actions. Philosopher Alasdair MacIntyre said that we cannot answer the question "What ought we to do?" until we know "Of which story are we a part?"[19] So, what story do we imagine we live in?

Consider this: There were highly calculated and diabolical reasons that loads of funding and ferocious energies were poured into the Third Reich's Ministry of Public Enlightenment and Propaganda. One of the first things Hitler did while rising to power was to brand, with his dehumanizing swastika, the imaginations of the people through stories told in film, theater, music, radio, print, and the press. Why? Because tyrants don't conquer only through marching armies but also through well-crafted narratives. Dictators have been deposed not only by swords but by sharply honed stories that enlist hearts. Empires have both ascended to clouds and been reduced to embers because of a tale well told. Nations are shaped

---

19 Alasdair MacIntyre, *After Virtue: A Study in Moral Theory,* 3rd ed. (University of Notre Dame Press, 2007), 216.

and reshaped by the imagination-sculpting power of narratives. It is as Austrian priest and philosopher Ivan Illich wrote:

> Neither revolution nor reformation can ultimately change a society, rather you must tell a new powerful tale, one so persuasive that it sweeps away the old myths and becomes the preferred story, one so inclusive that it gathers all the bits of our past and our present into a coherent whole, one that even shines some light into the future so that we can take the next step forward. If you want to change a society, then you have to tell an alternative story.[20]

So is it any wonder Jesus was a storyteller? Parables were the scalpels by which He went to surgery on cataracted hearts. Jesus changed the way people imagined the world and, therefore, how they would inhabit that world. He told stories because He was after our true humanity. "Look!" Jesus said. "See. Observe." If God's superabundance of love fashions the lilies of the field, then we should go about our days acting as though divine provision will come.[21] If it is indeed true that the heavenly Father surveys the horizon with a love-swollen heart, prepared to run toward the ragged prodigal, then how quickly we should turn to God in prayer after yet another shame-heaping self-destructive action.[22]

God the Father gladly greets us, so there is no cause for shame to keep us away. If God really came asking questions to

---

20 Jim Baumgaertel, "Storytelling or Myth-Making? Frank Viola and Ivan Illich," *Proclamation, Invitation, and Warning* (blog), December 13, 2018, procinwarn.com/counterfeit/storytelling.htm.

21 Matthew 6v25–34.

22 Luke 15v11–32.

draw Adam and Eve out from hiding behind the trees, we should engage God as the one who comes in gracious love to repair what we have ruptured. Having such a vision for reality should shape our behavior.

I wonder, what story of reality do our actions tell?

In His love for us, Jesus is after nothing less than the totality of how we perceive the world and how we participate in it. He is not after some abstract compartment within us called *belief.* He is not trying to install a new app called Christianity onto our old, glitching operating systems of self. He is about the work of giving us completely new operating systems. He is after our embodied being—our metabolisms, our synapses, our circadian rhythms, our lungs and thumbs, our glands and tongues.

Come and see, Jesus said. *Let your desires be reshaped by My love—and take up a life with Me.*

Now, with that groundwork on the faculty of the imagination, I think we are ready to explore how we see by way of the apprenticeship paradigm (Union → Abiding & Obeying → Imaging). Then, after exploring *how* we imagine apprenticeship in a healthy way, part two will get quite "bodily" as we examine the practices of how it is we inhabit this world like Jesus. First the paradigm, then the practices.

Come and see.

3

Fragments and Flourishing

On the Dynamics of Formation

He that breaks a thing to find out what it is has left the
path of wisdom.

—Gandalf the Grey, *The Fellowship of the Ring*

Ring the bells that still can ring
Forget your perfect offering
There is a crack, a crack in everything
That's how the light gets in.

—Leonard Cohen, "Anthem"

Have you ever felt a bit dragonish? Like there was something
beastly just beneath your skin? Greedy, steaming, scowling,
ready to devour others?

Or maybe you have felt phantomlike, insubstantial and
thin in soul, like mist or a shadow of some passing thing.
Have you ever experienced the uneasy feeling that something
is off deep in the architecture of who you are?

I am speaking here of that strange *off-ness* that is somehow
far more than the distinct feeling of having done something
wrong. No, this unease is something more unnerving, something deeper, something ancient. It is that unsettling sense
your very *being* is not quite right—and yet you can't quite put

your finger on where or what the off-ness is. It seems nowhere and everywhere.

In other words, have you ever felt less than human? Less than what you sense you ought to be? Less than what you want to be? Perhaps you're fighting off a sense of meaninglessness in your job. Maybe there's a gnawing ache in your relationships. Or an unease in your own skin. Do you feel some insistent ache to be something more? To be something brilliant and beautiful? Something lasting? To not feel like your days are wasted and who you are is of no consequence?

I have often felt this way—even while writing this book. I know quite well what it is like to grumble and skulk about in self-importance. To be clear, this ache is not just for romantics or for the melancholy soul. There is equal opportunity for existential ache here. Whether or not we have recognized it for what it really is, we have all felt the shiver of diminished humanity—the deep-seated haunt of being less than we should be.[1]

This is what Sylvia Plath was writing about in her journals when she said, "I am afraid. I am not solid, but hollow. I feel behind my eyes a numb, paralyzed cavern, a pit of hell, a mimicking nothingness. . . . I do not know who I am, where I am going."[2] Countless are the poems and songs and sighs and desperate acts for love that express similar groanings of the soul.

In a thousand ways, glittering and dark, graceful and

---

1 I realize that talk of "should be" and phrases like "the person you are meant to be" run counter to the grain of popular thought and will likely make some people uneasy or take offense. But herein lies the human problem. There is a dis-ease with what we are meant to be.

2 Sylvia Plath, *The Journals of Sylvia Plath* (Anchor, 1982), 60.

blundering, the human condition aches toward integration. We long for a happy fitting together of the bits and pieces of our humanity. For a mending of our many fractures. For an un-numbing and a reconnection. We reach for it in moments of resonance, in some experience of lust or power or being seen to make us feel all right.

A hungering for happy endings courses through us, running far deeper into our soul's strata than even our darkest cynical tendencies—and the dissonance of these longings and suspicions scrapes at us. Keeps us restless. Makes us homesick within our own homes loaded with customized comforts. Has us rattling about with anxiety. And so, we live in the tension, wondering *who* we are to be. *How* we are to be. *What* we are to be. Wondering why we are haunted by a ruthlessly elusive joy. Why something always seems to be missing. Why the good life is so hard to come by. All questions we ask even when we don't know we are asking them.

The Jim Carreys of the world who have reached nosebleed heights of fame warn us that golden awards and fawning followers and dreams-come-true still leave dark hollows in the soul (warnings we dismiss with eye rolls and "So says the guy who has it all!"). Things are not always how they appear. Happily married couples still crave a deeper sense of being known. Utopian communities end up as cults or nightmares on a real crime podcast. The vision of flourishing can seem like an ever-receding mirage that leads us farther into the barren wasteland.

The way of flourishing in a fragmented world is found in apprenticeship to Jesus. In union with Him, the one who holds all things together. A union that leads to abiding with Him and obeying Him, and results in imaging Him, becoming like Him degree by radiant degree. That is the central claim of this book: Apprenticeship to Jesus is the way of integration, a whole-life way of apprehending and existing in the world.

It is in Jesus that all the outward flying fragments find their place and cohere. Apprenticeship to Jesus is the *way*, the process of change by which image bearers of God become more like Jesus, *the truly human one*. The apostle Paul, throughout his many letters, obsessively taught that those who are "in Christ"[3] are becoming more like Him, are being "conformed to [His] image."[4] Because we are united to Jesus through His indwelling Spirit, "in Christ" we are living into the wonder of human nature as God has intended it to be. Becoming truly human.

But this beautiful truth is a medicine that many resist swallowing. The good news of becoming truly human tends to offend people in at least two ways.

First, some take offense at *becoming truly human* or *becoming more than we are* because in their estimation, "We are fine as we are, and, by the way, who is anyone to tell anyone else what they are to become? That's just another power play to control and colonize others." This view combines "you do you" with "who are you to tell me?" to arrive at the "authentic life." It chidingly tells others that the authentic self should not be challenged but must be validated and most certainly celebrated. This popularly peddled authentic life causes one to

---

3 In his thirteen letters, Paul talks of being "in Christ" or uses other similar phrases about union with Christ just over 160 times. It was of crucial importance for Paul to teach that our very being is bound up in Christ's being. This is the mystery of being "partakers of the divine nature" (2 Peter 1v4), a luminous mystery we'll look at later.

4 Romans 8v29.

gag at the slightest whiff of any authority outside of the self.[5] We'll address the curious tyranny of this not-so-self-aware view in just a bit.

There are others who take offense at the good news of the prospect of becoming truly human for a very different reason. There are some who believe it is our very humanity we need to escape. They declare, "The last thing we need is to be more human. We are all *too* human! We must transcend humanity!" In other words, they would like to read a book titled *Why We Need to Become Far Less Human Than We Currently Are.* But in my opinion, that sounds like a terrible book, not to mention that it is an abysmal misunderstanding of the storyline of Scripture.

I experienced this firsthand one Sunday morning when someone chafed at the sermon I had just preached on apprenticeship to Jesus and being rehumanized as we grow in Christlikeness. "My humanity is the problem—I need to get rid of me!" they passionately claimed. Their clear disdain for this thing called "humanity" and a projected self-loathing could not swallow the idea that Christ was the perfect human, because they believed our humanity is our enemy. "Jesus as God" was fully acceptable to them, but certainly He was not *truly* human. Surely Jesus had to rise above being human, not embody it!

The problem with this "escape from humanity" view is that humanity, in its very essence, is seen to be the problem. The patient *is* the disease. The child *is* the fever. The man *is* the cancer. But this is an odd sort of view when you take a

---

5 Often, when people speak of authenticity, what they mean is an "unaccountable life." But the two are quite different. We suffer from an imprecision in language.

long walk and think about it. Such a thought likely resides in the popular consciousness from the sticky old saying "To err is human," often attributed to English poet Alexander Pope.[6] But the saying comes from a much older source, namely the stoic philosopher Seneca the Younger, who was not known for having a biblical view of human nature.[7]

Is the essence of humanity "to err"? Is that really true?

I admit, the old saying has the sound of truth—but the truth is in the homophone: To *heir* is human. Our humanity is rooted in and realized through becoming like Jesus, the Son of God, the truly human one. It is crucial to understand that our problem is not in "being human"—the problem is a ruptured humanity, a vandalized and fractured nature. The problem is in our dis-integration, in our dehumanization.

In short, this kind of escape-from-humanity broken anthropology arises when one's understanding of human nature begins in Genesis chapter 3 as the garden grows shadowed and treacherous. But the Bible starts with chapter 1, not chapter 3. That is significant.

The biblical story begins with a generous, divine Giver, a song-singing Gardener who breathes out the splendors of existence, orders the elements, sets everything into its cosmic socket, and then stoops to get dark soil on His almighty hands. In short order, from His generative words, there is a wealth of goodness springing out of His fertile ground. Then, in this glorious origin story of humanity, heaven and earth

---

6 The phrase "To err is human; to forgive, divine" gained currency in the English language in 1711 after Alexander Pope's *An Essay on Criticism*.

7 *Errare humanum est, perseverare autem diabolicum, et tertia non datur* ("To err is human; to persist [in such errors] is of the devil, and the third possibility is not given"). Attributed to Seneca the Younger (c. 4 B.C.–A.D. 65).

intimately weave as this good God gladly breathes *His* breath into *His* man-shaped soil.

He calls this divinely inspired, bipedal, image-bearing wonder "very good." Not "meh." Not "that will suffice." Not even "good." But "very good." *Tov meod* in Hebrew.[8] *Tov meod*—those three syllables have a shimmering sound to them, don't they? *Very good* is there, upright and marvelous, right at the start of it all. Behold humanity—*the* magnificent creature! *Very good* is there long before the bent and vandalized version of humanity skulks in the shadows and starts throwing blame around.

So yes, the curse (the death that lurks about in our world) and our twistedness is a very real and present danger; it just turns out blessings are older than curses. Delight runs deeper than disruption. Beauty, goodness, and truth are primary; distortions, disorder, and fractures are only ever secondary at best. Evil is an interloper, not the homeowner. A parasite, not the party host. When we get these things mixed up, we confuse remedies and maladies.

The other challenge with this escape-from-humanity view is Jesus. Jesus is *fully* and *truly* human. In the incarnation, in the grand miracle of the Son of God coming in the flesh, being born of a virgin woman, He took on humanity not to obliterate it so we could escape it or transcend it, but so He could redeem it that we might live into its intended fullness. The eternal Son of God took on human nature in the person of Jesus to definitively show that heaven thought our dusty and cracked humanity was well worth putting back together again.

---

8 Strong's Hebrew Lexicon, "ṭôḇ," Blue Letter Bible, www.blueletterbible.org/lexicon/h2896/kjv/wlc/0-1; Strong's Hebrew Lexicon, "mᵊʿōḏ," Blue Letter Bible, www.blueletterbible.org/lexicon/h3966/kjv/wlc/0-1.

In other words, spiritual growth in this life, growth that leads to a greater sense of purpose and life, means becoming *more* human, not less. It means your humanity is recovered—it is being redeemed rather than discarded.

When His earthly work was done and He ascended to the Father, Jesus did not shed this humanity like some dirty work clothes tossed into the laundry. Jesus, with man-made scars marking His flesh-and-bone resurrected body, now rules over the cosmos. The blue-collar King now robed in splendor and light is still fully human and fully God. In fact, Jesus's favorite title for Himself in the Gospel accounts was the Son of Man—the human one.

Jesus did not hold His divine nose in disgust when He assumed humanity—rather, *He embodied humanity as humanity is intended to be.* Who Jesus was and is ought to conclusively tell us that our humanity is a good gift to be honored and restored, not an unfavorable thing to be tossed out, not a curse to be broken. The curse is in weaponizing the good gift against the generous Giver and becoming more and more dehumanized in doing so.

And this, dear reader, means that your creator and redeemer doesn't want to obliterate you. He wants you to be more truly you, the true self He envisaged in His love and perfection—not some neutralized, generic carbon copy of someone else. He is not after some dystopian *Handmaid's Tale* version of you. The beautiful complexity of who you are—your temperament, your story, your epigenetics,[9] your uniqueness that was fearfully and wonderfully knit together

---

9 Epigenetics is the study of how environmental factors and lifestyle choices influence the way genes function (how they are turned on or off), which can lead to lasting effects on an organism's traits and health.

in your mother's womb[10]—is brought closer to its design as you are conformed to the image of Christ. Like sunlight pouring into a dark room, the Light brings out the colors and shapes and beautifying contrasts; it does not bleach them all to non-distinction.

AREN'T WE ALL TRULY HUMAN?

Now, I realize a question may arise fairly quickly. I used the words *truly human*. But aren't we all human? What's with the "truly" bit? It sounds a little judgy. A bit dodgy. Maybe even dangerous (possible fodder for some new tyranny or eugenics project!). It is very much the opposite. So let me clear this up before strange suspicions grow.

We are all fully human, yes, but not all are *truly* human.

Wait—what? How is that? I will try to explain, as it is important for understanding spiritual formation.

The call to be truly human is not some justification for superiority of one person over another, nor is it some bizarre transhumanist dream ideated amid the glass-walled offices of Silicon Valley; rather, it is the paradoxical common sense that in some real way, each and every day, we feel we are not as we ought to be. I am referring here to the idea that we all live in a story not yet finished, a narrative yearning for resolution, a tale seeking some happily-ever-after, bits and pieces longing for meaningful cohesion. The Bible shows us that we are a people *in medias res*.[11] We are mid-story people. Longings,

---

10 Psalm 139v14–16.
11 Latin for "in the middle of things."

hopes, and haunts make up the curves, corners, and corridors of our eternity-shaped hearts.[12] Human beings are all in process—meant to mature, to live into our intended design.

Simply put, there is room for growth. For everyone. For me. For you. For the hermit monk who has exhibited decades of Herculean discipline. For the saintliest octogenarian who has yet to miss a Sunday service. For the theologian with a double PhD. On the maps of all our souls there are dark oceans labeled "Here be dragons."[13] There remain chaotic regions of our being that need to be charted and named by love.

The fact that every human being is an in-process image bearer of God means that every one of us is in a process of spiritual formation—atheist, Buddhist, Stoic, Neoplatonist, anarchist, Baptist, *Star Wars* enthusiast, anime or baseball fanatic. If you are breathing, you are being formed—or being de-formed. We are malleable creatures with neuroplastic minds and woo-able hearts, created to be conformed to what is beautiful, good, and true.

There is an indelible twin law of humanity: *We become like what we behold* and *Behavior is becoming*.[14] Consciously or unconsciously, you are becoming a person of greater or lesser love and joy through your attentions and actions. We

---

12 Ecclesiastes 3v11.

13 Medieval mapmakers had a practice of putting the Latin phrase *hic sunt dracones* ("Here be dragons") and/or illustrations of dragons, sea monsters, or other mythological creatures on areas of maps where unexplored territories and potential dangers were thought to exist.

14 The phrase "we become like what we behold" is often attributed to Marshall McLuhan due to the general idea being prevalent in his work. Going back to an older source, the poet William Blake wrote in his 1804 poem *Milton,* "Terrified Los stood in the Abyss & his immortal limbs / Grew deadly pale; he became what he beheld." The person called Los in the poem is a personification of the human imagination.

are on our way to being either "immortal horrors or everlasting splendors," as C. S. Lewis wrote.[15] Or as Robert Mulholland, Jr., explained,

> *Everyone* is in a process of spiritual formation! . . . We are being shaped into either the wholeness of the image of Christ or a horribly destructive caricature of that image, destructive not only to ourselves but also to others, for we inflict our brokenness upon them. . . . The direction of our spiritual growth infuses all we do with intimations of either life or death.[16]

And so, the word *truly* here means rightly, correctly, or genuinely. It is used to mean "in accordance with one's nature and purpose." It is a word that weaves together the realities of design and destiny, purpose and potential, process and possibility. We are not static beings that just are. We are not past-tense beings all buttoned up. We are beings given an ineradicable calling of becoming. Becoming what we ought to become. Now, *there's* a controversial word—*ought*. You could say that there is a massive "ought to" that smiles over our lives. It is a love-bearing and joy-bringing ought, not some oppressive burden, some uncaring cosmic demand that steals from us. This oughtness to existence has to do with being free as only a human being can be free. G. K. Chesterton expressed this wonderfully when he said,

---

15 C. S. Lewis, *The Weight of Glory and Other Addresses* (HarperOne, 1980), 46.

16 M. Robert Mulholland, Jr., *Invitation to a Journey: A Road Map for Spiritual Formation* (InterVarsity, 2016), 27–28.

You can free things from alien or accidental laws, but not from the laws of their own nature. You may, if you like, free a tiger from his bars; but do not free him from his stripes. Do not free a camel of the burden of his hump: you may be freeing him from being a camel.[17]

Yet, more and more, we keep trying to free tigers from their stripes, and it is a dangerous endeavor. And modern culture's proclivity for trying to liberate camels from their humps is flat-out cruel. To free humans from the happy oughts of delighting in God's Word and the design of His world, from loving God and from loving others, from biological design, is to free them from being human. It is to free them from the way of flourishing by unleashing a riot of dis-integrating forces. In the great ravaging of the human imagination, we dis-imagine the world, deny a meaning-giving Creator, and disavow nature, saying this one thing can be any other thing if only we want it to be so.

Not so.

Any zoologist would defend a camel being a camel if you were to ignore its hump and call it a horse or house cat. But when it comes to human beings, well, Western culture views human beings as sentient modeling clay—biological markers meaning nothing of real consequence. So, a man might be a woman if a will wants it, a woman a man if that is the rising desire, or a person a thing, given "it" is only a strange accident of atoms and meaningless twists of DNA in a world that is "just stuff" all the way down. But this world is not

---

17 G. K. Chesterton, *Orthodoxy* (Dodd, Mead, 1908), 71–72.

just stuff that we can do whatever with without reaping consequences.

The world is filled with unassailable oughts, which we need to realize are actually "get to's" baked into creation. They are not oppressive commands that kill the party, but are instead an invitation to live in the glad and luminous ways of reality. They set dislocated hearts back into their sockets. As H. H. Farmer said, "If you go against the grain of the universe, you get splinters."[18] Turns out cosmic splinters hurt—a lot. My news feed reminds me of this daily with images of a war-ravaged Middle East.

To be truly human is to live in a way that is true to our design and purpose—that is, to live *in accordance with reality.* And until we do, we will be puzzled by the pieces of our lives. We are to live and to love in accordance with what is most true about the world. *That* is freedom. To be a person of God-born love and joy.[19] To be truly human is to be congruent—for the fragments of our lives to wonderfully fit and to flourish in the love of God that holds all things together. Of course, not all people live in accordance with reality. I don't think it a bit controversial to say that many are not people of increasing love and joy. I imagine you could name at least a few people who need more love and joy in their life. We all know a few sour curmudgeons and soul-sucking cynics. (And if not, well, *we* just might be one.)

---

18 Eugene H. Peterson, *A Long Obedience in the Same Direction: Discipleship in an Instant Society,* 20th anniversary ed. (InterVarsity, 2000), 121.

19 Paul tells us in Romans 5v5 that "hope does not put us to shame, because God's love has been poured into our hearts through the Holy Spirit who has been given to us."

There is a great deal of unreality prowling about, ready to suck the joy and lifeblood out of any room—and it's not just on social media; it's at work and in our homes and in our hearts. It seems that a shadow side of being creatures made in the image of an infinite God is that we are capable of "infinite self-delusion."[20] We think we are just fine while we bleed out.[21]

Take a moment to scroll through your news feed and watch the injustices of the world glow on your screen. Let the algorithm testify to our own distorted desires as it reflects in greater proportions the darkness hidden in our hearts. Simply rewatch a violent newsclip and the AI feeds you back three more atrocities. A quick Google search reveals troubling stats on loneliness, depression, anxiety, and self-harm.

- A recent study by Cigna reports that Generation Z (ages 18–22) is the loneliest generation, with 79 percent reporting feelings of loneliness.[22]
- Anxiety and depression increased by 63 percent in young adults in the US from 2005 to 2017.[23]

---

20 Gertrude Atherton, *Adventures of a Novelist* (Jonathan Cape, 1932), 255.

21 Often, we simply can't see that we are like the absurd Black Knight from *Monty Python and the Holy Grail*—the one who is tragicomically proud and terribly self-unaware and so keeps calling out, "It's a mere flesh wound!" while his limbs are lopped off one by bloody one.

22 Jessica Buechler, "The Loneliness Epidemic Persists: A Post-Pandemic Look at the State of Loneliness Among U.S. Adults," The Cigna Group, accessed January 18, 2025, newsroom.thecignagroup.com/loneliness-epidemic -persists-post-pandemic-look.

23 Emma Kauana Osorio and Emily Hyde, "The Rise of Anxiety and Depression Among Young Adults in the United States," Ballard Brief, Winter 2021, ballardbrief.byu.edu/issue-briefs/the-rise-of-anxiety-and-depression-among -young-adults-in-the-united-states.

- Anxiety among children (ages 3–17) increased 27 percent from 2016 to 2019.[24]
- There was a 30 percent increase in suicide in the US from 2000 to 2016.[25]

All is not well. Yet we say, "I'm fine, I'm fine!" And so . . .

Can we agree that there are certain ways of being, of inhabiting this world, that are healthier or better or more humane than others? Ways of being that are more beautiful, good, and true? If not, then there is no sound basis for any form of education, no foundation for any law, no logic for logic, no reason for reason, no good sense for discourse, debate, discipline, honor, or celebration. There's no foundation from which to discuss politics, sexuality, gender, or to ask anyone to affirm anything. No reason to virtue signal or cancel someone or drag their name through social media mud.

If there are not better ways of inhabiting this world, all that is left is a mire of shifting preferences wielded in the madness of some Nietzschean power struggle (which may be philosophically stimulating to think about, but a world no one would actually vote for). If that is not the case, then this book, along with every book ever written, is just more hapless noise amid the sound and fury of a meaningless life.[26] Best cut your losses now, toss this aside, and go do something devilishly fun.

---

24 Osorio and Hyde, "The Rise of Anxiety."

25 Osorio and Hyde, "The Rise of Anxiety."

26 A reference to Macbeth's oh-so-cheery lines "Life's but a walking shadow, a poor player / That struts and frets his hour upon the stage / And then is heard no more. It is a tale / Told by an idiot, full of sound and fury / Signifying nothing." *Macbeth,* act 5, scene 5, lines 27–31.

Let's use a small but mighty word here that our world needs: *telic*.[27] We are telic creatures. Think *tele*scope or *tele*vision, *tele*phone or *tele*gram. That *tele* bit has to do with something reaching its far aim, its intended goal. We are creatures with a nature oriented toward an intended end. We are meaningful beings. We can't escape that—and we are relentlessly haunted if we try. We are less like an inert rock and more like arrows crafted, drawn, aimed, and fired at a target. Our lives have velocity and are thus always aimed at something (or someone). We have a telos.[28] This means that becoming is essential to who we are—which makes a load of sense if, in fact, we are finite beings made in the image of an infinite and eternal God. This means we are all in the process of formation.

Now, that sounds a bit abstract, so let's think about something a little more earthy, more bodily, to grasp how *becoming* is at the heart of spiritual formation.

ON FORMATION (A CHILD IS VERY NON-ABSTRACT)

Think of a child. A child is very non-abstract—all flesh and bone and writhing wants and curious smells and glorious giggles. From conception, they are human. Nestled in the womb, that child is a human being. A person. At birth that child is a human being. As a toddler stumbling about like a drunken sailor, they are a human being. As an emboldened

---

27 *Telic* means "directed toward an end; purposeful." *Collins Dictionary*, "telic," accessed April 25, 2025, www.collinsdictionary.com/us/dictionary/english/telic.

28 *Telos* is a Greek word for "end, goal, or purpose." Strong's Greek Lexicon, "telos," Blue Letter Bible, www.blueletterbible.org/lexicon/g5056/kjv/tr/0-1.

twenty-year-old whose prefrontal cortex is still neurologically coalescing, they are a human being. At midlife, when crisis comes calling and hair starts silvering, still human. In the golden years, when the shadows of memories are long and energies short, still a precious human being. At ninety-nine and in a nursing home, most certainly still a human being, no matter how ageist our society has become. Regardless of age or stage, that human being is ever on a journey of being formed. How could it be otherwise for a finite and time-bound creature whose heart's chambers hold eternal splendors and ancient shadows?

Think of the colossal potential tightly curled up within that child while in their mother's belly or cradled in her arms. Imagine the wonders of humanity that are waiting to be released, unfurled, revealed, and reveled in as that child experiences the wild things of the world, steps forward into wider horizons of possibility, forms relationships, navigates suffering, and delights in the joys of being known. The child's experiences and memories deepen and widen like reaching roots, while their opportunities and outcomes expand and stretch upward like the branches of a great oak toward the light of the sun. Purpose, potential, and possibility all woven together in this small being who *is* and who *is becoming*. No wonder the literary genius Isaiah wrote of God's people, "They will be called oaks of righteousness, a planting of the LORD for the display of his splendor."[29]

That child is fully human from the start, yet they are growing into their true humanity, degree by degree, heading toward their pregnant potential. Their very *being* is a *becom-*

---

29 Isaiah 61v3, NIV.

ing. Their faculties, their facets of soul, their potential and destiny are all being integrated through inhabiting time. It is a *now and not yet* kind of thing. And so it is with apprenticeship to Jesus.

As apprentices to Jesus, we are those born anew, with a line of crimson and gold life dawning in our dark hearts. We are human beings becoming something wonderful as we are being conformed to the image of Jesus. In every apprentice of Jesus, truly, something wonderful this way comes.[30] Day has come and is coming. We are a now and not yet people.

In other words, human beings have an ontological potential—we are to become who we truly are.[31] That is not a typo; it is a hopeful truth. Take heart. We can change.

We can change.

The frayed pieces of our being can meet and weave. We are those who, like a seed, are latent with life, with a forest of flourishing all coiled up within something small and unassuming. And who we truly are has everything to do with our origin, our essence, and our aim. These things are given to us—they are not achieved but bestowed upon us by our creator. No one authors their own origin story. No child conceives themselves or decides where they're born. No creature invents its essence or engineers its intended aim. These things are the jurisdiction of the Creator. These things are to be re-

---

30 As a little kid I was haunted by the movie version of Ray Bradbury's novel *Something Wicked This Way Comes.* I think what struck me most was the title itself (which is a line from Shakespeare's *Macbeth*), as it invoked in me an intense longing to watch or to read or to someday write a story called *Something Wonderful This Way Comes.* There was an ache for a beauty that would outshine the carnivalesque and creepy.

31 *Ontological* relates to the branch of metaphysics dealing with the nature of being and existence.

ceived and celebrated. They are *givens*. We are God's beloved creatures, He has finely crafted our nature, and He has brilliantly designed not only our *who* and our *what,* but the *how* that makes for our flourishing.

A creature, by definition, is never its own creator. We are each bestowed with a what, a why, and a how. And the *how* is Jesus and a life of apprenticeship to Him. He is the Way. We don't get to make up our own way to be human. As the psalmist wrote:

> Teach me your way, O LORD,
>> that I may walk in your truth;
>> unite my heart to fear your name. (86v11)

This means that the good news of our creatureliness is that we are free of the burden of having to be our own god.

Take that in for a moment with a sigh of relief.

We are not bound to the impossible and dread-inducing task of creating meaning for our lives. This divine weight is crushing for human shoulders. Meaning is a treasure excavated, discovered—it is not invented or fabricated like new technology. Freedom is found in being conformed to the image of God. An image bearer is free only when they are imaging their creator. Liberate them of that and, well, it is the madness of emancipating a star from its light or unshackling the sparrow from its wings. As the apostle Paul penned, "Where the Spirit of the Lord is, there is freedom."[32] And it is through the empowering presence of the Spirit that we can become like Jesus and know flourishing.

---

32 2 Corinthians 3v17.

THE "S" WORD

Of course, there is that which we could call *not-freedom,* or *not-wholeness.* There is that which misshapes us. Unfortunately, there is an awful lot of this not-freedom and not-wholeness on the loose. There is a mutinous shatteredness to our being that works to undo us, to subvert us. There is a dis-integrating force at work in the world called—dare I say it?—sin.

It is a massively unpopular (though helpful) word, this little word *sin.* Sin is not just out there in systems and organizations and clandestine societies. This dis-integrating force is in *you.* In *me.* Interlaced into the fibers of our agency. It is in our very own bodies, woven into our histories. Paul often calls it our *flesh.*

Sin vandalizes the intended beauty of humanity. It is an agent of chaos. It pollutes and it pulls apart. It is like a moral rust, an ethical cancer. It glitches the wonder of our origin, our essence, and our aim. It is a dark pattern that turns us against ourselves and everyone else.[33] Again, just take a brief scroll through your social feed or do a quick audit of your own unvarnished thoughts today. Or look over your relationships. There are scars and shrapnel we carry. Clearly, all is not well.

One of the great observable facts of existence is that the world around and within us groans. Why? The groaning speaks of an intended state, a properly ordered integration of the fragments now chafing in friction. If not, then the groaning, the suffering all around us, is only a kind of fic-

---

33 *Dark pattern* is a name given to a user interface that has been meticulously designed to trick users into doing things that will have unwanted consequences.

tion. That, in my opinion, is a hard sell—calling suffering a fiction, saying the groaning signifies nothing about what should be. No, the suffering is every bit real, and so the shadow proves the sunshine.[34] The pain in a dislocated shoulder speaks of the goodness of being in socket. The groaning is a servant of flourishing, preaching to us that there is a way of integration, a wholeness to be had, and we are not there yet.

It is important for us to realize that sin is not the religious name given to the stuff that is fun but that God has ungenerously decided He doesn't want us to do for some prudish or killjoy reason. Sin is that which dehumanizes us. It is thought, word, or deed that dismantles our integrity and sabotages flourishing. Sin is soul irrationality. It is that which refuses what is *really* real. Sin is rupture, disorder.

But what is sin? Its essence is *autonomy*.[35] What does this mean? In short, self-rule. It means attempting to be truly human or to be "like God" on one's own terms.[36] Attempting to hold the universe together with our own breakable hands. It is not trusting the Creator, who has given you every reason to trust Him, but instead trusting a strange trash-talking creature in the blooming garden that God has given you to enjoy. It is attempting to define for ourselves what is good and what is bad, as though we are the authors of the world into which we came with a blur and blood, kicking and crying. To be an image bearer and refuse the One whose image you exist in is to sabotage one's own flourishing. It is to chainsaw the branch upon which you stand, flexing and bragging while you eat of

---

34 Thank you, Jon Foreman and Switchfoot.

35 A smart-sounding word that means "a law unto oneself."

36 Genesis 3v5.

the tree's fruit. It is, as Jesus once said, to build one's house on sand.[37] All that does not proceed from trust in God is sin.[38]

As I heard my father say countless times over the years: "Don't go shooting yourself in the foot and then wondering why it hurts." But we are a trigger-happy lot of limping people, aren't we?

BITS AND PIECES

Now, if it is true that apprenticeship to Jesus is the way of human flourishing as the Scriptures show and tell (and as we will see), then knowing *what* apprenticeship to Jesus is and *how* it happens seems rather important and worth a few pages of spilled ink. But to address this well, we need to examine the state of the world in which we live. A proper diagnosis is necessary for a wise remedy.

We live in a dis-integrated age, a world cleft and fractured in countless ways. A world of splintered light in which the colors of the spectrum are weaponized against one another. Some years ago, Francis Schaeffer offered the grave diagnosis that "the basic problem of the Christians in this country in the last eighty years or so, in regard to society and in regard to government, is that they have seen things in bits and pieces instead of totals."[39] Far too often, we go about our days gathering a smattering of our preferred pixels rather than delighting in the totality of the wider image. Reductive tendencies

---

37 Matthew 7v26–27.

38 Romans 14v23.

39 Francis A. Schaeffer, *A Christian Manifesto* (Crossway, 1982), 17–18.

abound. Benevolent tensions are systematically severed. Polarization is pop culture's way.

Schaeffer does not simply diagnose a problem in the American church, but peers into the very heart of the human crisis: dis-integration. He catches a glimpse of the raw edges of the fragmented self.[40] He gets right to the heart of the troubled human condition. Schaeffer has exposed how deep the discipleship crisis in the Western church really runs. I use the word *crisis* not to frighten or catastrophize—there's quite enough of that in every news feed—but to simply say that there is a deep and dark malady at hand, and that there is a better way.

The word *crisis* means to come to a decision point, a place of separation or divide, and it is often used to speak of the turning point in a disease that leads either to recovery or death. Likewise, our approach to apprenticeship to Jesus leads either to recovery or death, flourishing or further dis-integration of our being. How we imagine apprenticeship to Jesus has consequences.

All too often the dis-integration at work in the world is just as vigorously at work within the church, pulling things apart and pitting good thing against good thing with reductive and destructive either/ors: grace or effort, rest or activity, truth or gentleness, justice or mercy, self or community, being known or being loved. And though the church at large traffics in vast quantities of Christian content, it often does so in unseen reductive ways, buying into the darkest shadows of

---

40 This fragmented self is one that is alienated from God, from others, from self, and from creation. Let's call these four alienations "the four fractures of the fall." Sin fragmented every possible human relationship.

the Enlightenment project that reduced humans to machinery. Bits and pieces. Shards and fragments. The result is that most people do not have an integrative narrative about apprenticeship to Jesus and how it leads to flourishing.

We live in a world with a vast cultural architecture that is ever grinding and churning, its metal and wheels clacking and turning to coerce us into the "great freedom" of self-creation. Billions of dollars and brain cells are spent each year fueling the attention economy, telling us over and over that we must forge our own way of being human. This manifesto is shouted and whispered—embedded into images, written into scripts, and encoded into algorithms: *Make yourselves! Invent you! Be true to yourself, follow your desires (whatever they are today, however they may change tomorrow), and above all, never forget to publish your identity! Post it. Brand it. Relentlessly broadcast that curated self for clicks of validation. Anything less is oppression, tyranny, and the colonization of your soul.* It's all very exhausting.

Call it expressive individualism.[41] Call it the sovereign self or the cult of authenticity, or call it all a bit confusing—but in the Western world it is the very air we breathe, the pervasive cultural imagination that animates the posts in our feeds and energizes the tales told in our growing Netflix queue.

We are apprentices to ourselves. And this self-authoring spirit of the age is inherently entropic, dismantling, and destructive.

---

41 Expressive individualism is the view that the point of a person's existence is to be authentic. For individuals to be authentic, they must align their lives with their desires; and for societies to be authentic, they must applaud individuals for aligning life with their desires. (For an excellent scholarly treatment of expressive individualism and its genealogy, read Carl Trueman's *The Rise and Triumph of the Modern Self*.)

This design-your-own-way-of-being-human mentality is a snake eating its own tail. It is a broken cistern leaking water, not the spring of living water the PR machine says it is. It is reductive and alienating, at work grinning and grinding, making more bits and pieces of the bits and pieces of us (*ahem,* identity politics and its exponential energies of subdividing). It is essentially competitive, agonistic, us versus them (defining the self against and over others). When there is no shared narrative, no common drama or integrating story arc over our lives, then there are only innumerable competing micronarratives that can never cohere; they simply collide and chip bits off one another like poorly packed dishes in a moving box.

This pervasive way of the self-made self, of our identity creation quest, is deeply at odds with apprenticeship to Jesus. It is simply not Christian, and by *Christian* I mean *the way of Jesus.* Yet in the Western church, following Jesus is often just another way to "create oneself." Apprenticeship is often hijacked and jury-rigged as another piece in assembling a customized self. But apprenticeship to Jesus is not some technique for self-creation.

That is the malady, so what is the remedy?

Apprenticeship to Jesus is something wholly *other*—something countercultural and a fundamentally different way of inhabiting the world. Something subversive to the rampant cult of self-creation. It is the grace-born and fully embodied process of being conformed into the likeness of our creator through His empowering presence. It is the kingdom of heaven taking on flesh on earth.

What we need is a rightly storied imagination of what it means to become truly human. We require an integrated and accessible vision of the origin, the essence, and the aim of apprenticeship to help us re-imagine apprenticeship and re-inhabit the world in light of it. This, I should note again, is the way of spiritual formation: the mutually reinforcing interplay of a *renewed imagination* and *renovating habits* that write the truth of reality into our bodies amid the humdrum of daily life. The kingdom of God needs to get into our bodies, into our bones, into our myelin sheathing.[42] Apprenticeship is not an abstraction; it lives and breathes in what we practice. It is "bodied forth" in the process of being conformed to the image of the truly human one—Jesus Christ.

But before we look more directly into the apprenticeship paradigm and its practices, we still have some things to address with the bits and pieces of a fractured world. We live in the Age of Dis-Integration. We should be conscious of its deforming ways and have an idea of why we are haunted in the ways we are haunted.

---

42 Myelin is a sheathlike material that forms an insulating and protective coating around nerve fibers. Myelination is a physiological process that occurs when a new neural pathway and habit is being formed.

4

The Age of Dis-Integration

A Heap of Broken Images

What are the roots that clutch, what branches grow
Out of this stony rubbish? Son of man,
You cannot say, or guess, for you know only
A heap of broken images, where the sun beats,
And the dead tree gives no shelter, the cricket no relief,
And the dry stone no sound of water.
                              —T. S. Eliot, *The Waste Land*

For the world is broken, sundered, busted down the
middle, self ripped from self and man pasted back together
as mythical monster, half angel, half beast, but no man.
                              —Walker Percy, *Love in the Ruins*

A longing for a home we have never been to. The call of a
strange nostalgia, of pasts not yet had, memories not yet
made. Glimmers of some bright sorrow that run us through.
The sense of being joy-haunted. Brazilians call it *saudade*. The
Welsh refer to it as *hiraeth*. Germans know it as *sehnsucht*—
a word C. S. Lewis was quite fond of.[1] For the Swedes it is

---

1 "Lewis described *Sehnsucht* as the 'inconsolable longing' in the human heart
for 'we know not what.'" Gregory S. Cootsona, *C. S. Lewis and the Crisis of a
Christian* (Presbyterian Publishing, 2014), 46. In the afterword of his book *The*

vemod. Such words are attempts to name the traces of Eden we carry within us. Echoes of our origin and destiny. Welcome to the brilliance and the brokenness of being human.

As I write these words, Elon Musk has just launched xAI, an artificial intelligence project with the aim to "understand the true nature of the universe"—yet another bid to understand this world and humanity's place within it. And in the wake of the acclaimed film *Oppenheimer,* director Christopher Nolan has said, "Artificial intelligence researchers refer to the present moment as an 'Oppenheimer moment.'"[2] He claims the film's story is a "warning" to a world that must wrestle with artificial intelligence and what it means for us to be human in an AI world. Interestingly, and profoundly interconnected, Greta Gerwig's highly acclaimed film *Barbie* launched the same weekend as *Oppenheimer,* igniting a bizarre and buzzworthy mashup of popular interest and existential exploration that was dubbed Barbenheimer. Amid the palette of pastels and fiery pink, Barbie and Ken wrestle with gender politics while on the journey from Barbieland to the Real World—an odyssey of realizing their personhood. In an odyssey warning us of silicon minds and plastic people, the box office yet again asks, What does it mean to be truly human? We cannot escape the question: Who are we?

Or, for our purposes, perhaps the even more important question is: Who or what are we becoming?

Pilgrim's Regress, Lewis wrote of this inconsolable longing as "that unnameable something, desire for which pierces us like a rapier at the smell of a bonfire, the sound of wild ducks flying overhead, the title of *The Well at the World's End,* the opening lines of *Kubla Khan,* the morning cobwebs in late summer, or the noise of falling waves" (Eerdmans, 1943), 237.

2 Laura Guitar, "Of Artificial Intelligence and Ants," rbb Communications, January 26, 2024, https://rbbcommunications.com/blog/of-ai-and-ants.

Anthropology is the viral question of the day, the prevailing question of our age.[3] Who are we? What does it mean to be human? These questions are ancient, yet uniquely amplified in our digital age. The energy and prevalence with which these questions are asked has reached higher registers in a world abuzz about ChatGPT and the rising tide of all things AI. Anthropology is glowing on our screens and flickering in our feeds. It is humming in our Spotify playlists and our Netflix queues. Anthropology is there to be seen in the algorithms pursuing and mapping the patterns of our attentions. It is on the move in our politics and our virtue signaling, on display under the bright lights and scalpels of transgenderism.

Don't let the fancy word intimidate you. Anthropology is a way of talking about the relentless impulse that seeks to answer the question, What does it mean to be truly human?[4] This is the never-ending question we are asking even when we are completely unaware we are asking it. The quest for our identity is humming under the skin of most everything, like some invisible current that animates the world in which we live. It is the inquiry we cannot escape.

The question of anthropology oozes like oil out of all we are and do. We are all anthropologists, in a sense. It is why we watch the movies we do; it is why we devour the delicious morsels of Monday-morning gossip about our co-workers. We don't need an academic degree or job title for this to be true. And this anthropological oozing has everything to do

3 This is not the only question we face, of course. But it does seem that certain ages, certain periods of history are marked by key questions and core concerns that capture the zeitgeist, the spirit of the age.

4 *Anthropology* literally means "human study." *Anthropos* is Greek for man or human, and the *ology* bit comes from the Greek word *logos,* which means "reason" and/or "study of."

with God. We cannot know what it means to be truly human without knowing God, for the paradox of our humanness is we cannot know ourselves without knowing and being known by others. This is why John Calvin, the well-known theologian reformer of the church, began his classic work *The Institutes of the Christian Religion* with the famous sentence "Our wisdom, insofar as it ought to be deemed true and solid wisdom, consists almost entirely of two parts: the knowledge of God and of ourselves."[5] The order is intentional—it is in knowing God that we have the light necessary to see ourselves.

Anthropology needs theology. Self-knowledge needs a light from beyond itself. No matter how close one stands to a mirror intent on seeing their own face, there is simply no seeing the self in a lightless room. The light must be turned on. We are only groping around in the dark if we go about seeking our humanity without attending to God.

Even at the most basic sociological and psychological levels, we learn who we are in relationship with others. Our social interactions are like explorations that not only map the terrain of our soul but participate in shaping the very landscape of who we are. The warm hospitality of a new friend unfolds rolling hills and spreads new horizon lines within us. A lover's look strikes our heart's sea with sudden sunlight, bringing it to life and exposing unseen life swimming within. A parent's abuse carves sharp chasms, traumatizing our soul's bedrock. A peer's cold shoulder, like a late-season frost, withers young fruit and deadens green leaves.

Who we are, our identity, is shaped in, by, and through

---

5 John Calvin, *Institutes of the Christian Religion,* trans. Henry Beveridge (Peabody, 2008), 1.

relationships. In ubuntu, a foundational African philosophy, there is a saying in Zulu: *Umuntu ngumuntu ngabantu.*[6] It means "a person is a person through persons." Alpha male, John Wayne–like individualism is a Western lie. We need less John Wayne and more John Donne, the poet-priest who wrote:

> No man is an island, entire of itself; every man is a piece of the continent, a part of the main. If a clod be washed away by the sea, Europe is the less, as well as if a promontory were, as well as if a manor of thy friend's or of thine own were: any man's death diminishes me, because I am involved in mankind, and therefore never send to know for whom the bells tolls; it tolls for thee.[7]

Maybe you have heard of *interpersonal neurobiology.* It is a newer interdisciplinary framework that integrates research from independent disciplines into an understanding of how the brain and mind are shaped in the context of relationships.[8] In short, it explores how we are *embodied* beings, *embedded* in intricate webs of social relationships, *enacted* or *encoded* through experiences (shaped by our experiences of the world that now shape how we experience the world), and *extended* beings (our inner world affects the outer world and forms the

---

6 The phrase is sometimes translated "I am because we are." *Ubuntu* is a Nguni Bantu term meaning "humanity."

7 John Donne, *Devotions upon Emergent Occasions Together with Death's Duel,* ed. Andrew Motion (Ann Arbor, 1959), 108–9.

8 Interpersonal neurobiology (IPNB) is also called relational neuroscience. It was developed by Daniel J. Siegel in the 1990s. For further study, see the works of Dr. Curt Thompson, who does a marvelous job bringing together IPNB and biblical anthropology.

artifacts around us, and these artifacts then shape the ways in which we think).[9] These are new terms that walk age-old paths. Long before interpersonal neurobiology stepped on the scene, the doctrine of the Trinity taught that knowing and being known are at the deep heart of existence. God is a community within Himself, and we are inexorably relational beings made in His image.

We cannot know ourselves without knowing others—and the ultimate other is the Creator. The ultimate other is God. Who we truly are is found only in Him. Until we meet with Him, we will never truly meet ourselves, only shifting shadows and hazy phantoms of our real identity. Until we have fellowship with this Ultimate Other, we will experience alienation from our very selves. And so, in a world thirsting for anthropological answers while refusing to include God in the search for self, we are like castaways drinking salt water. We will only increase our thirst by what we are swallowing. Our consuming efforts burn us up from the inside out, getting us no closer to soul refreshing. The more we clamor toward authentic humanity without turning to apprenticeship to Jesus, the more frantic and violent and fractional we become.

We live in the Age of Dis-Integration, and the compounding dis-integration that is around and within us is at work diminishing and distorting our humanity. Just as the Agricul-

---

9 These are the four E's of what is called 4E cognition. James Carney, "Thinking Avant la Lettre: A Review of 4E Cognition," *Evolutionary Studies in Imaginative Culture* 4, no. 1 (2020): 77–90, www.ncbi.nlm.nih.gov/pmc/articles /PMC7250653; Albert Newen, Shaun Gallagher, and Leon De Bruin, "4E Cognition: Historical Roots, Key Concepts, and Central Issues," *The Oxford Handbook of 4E Cognition,* Oxford Library of Psychology (2018; online ed., Oxford Academic), 3–16, academic.oup.com/edited-volume/28083/chapter -abstract/212118698.

tural Age gave way to the Industrial Age, and the Industrial Age gave rise to the Information Age, the Information Age has given way to the Age of Dis-Integration: a period of history that is profoundly marked by the widespread dismantling and dis-integration of *story, people, place,* and *time.*

This is not to say things haven't always been breaking down from Genesis 3 onward—they have. Painfully so. But it is to say that our age is a curious amplifier to the dis-integrating force of sin. The cultural moment we find ourselves in is peculiarly adept at fracturing those things that lead to human flourishing. Just as echoes have been a natural occurrence in canyons throughout all of existence, human dis-integration has been a constant since the fall. But like the technology of a microphone and sound system, which can create a destructive feedback loop, the machinations of our age have become a particularly powerful amplifier that takes soft signals and splinters eardrums with it.

Grant me a moment for some not-so-cheery sociocultural analysis that will help us navigate the landscape in which we are following the way of Jesus. It is crucial we diagnose these problems for the sake of counter-formation and our healing.

SIX DIS-INTEGRATIONS

This Age of Dis-Integration we find ourselves in is marked by being *disenchanted, dissociated, discontextualized, dislocated, disembodied,* and *disconnected.* How is that for a happy list? It might not be happy, but it is helpful in diagnosing what is going on. Becoming aware of the forces that deform us will help us in following the way of Jesus.

1. The Age of Dis-Integration Is a *Disenchanted* Age

Ours is a world deeply formed by centuries of secular forces. A world in which self-sure human reason has long attempted to exile God and banish the supernatural to the realm of fiction and superstition—all things are to be only and ever explained by sheer material causes. Meaning exists only within human minds that must create it for themselves (because there is simply no inherent meaning to discover in an accidental world). Thus it is a world in which ultimate authority is now relocated within the individual self. Morality is a matter of opinion rather than transcendent truth. Facts are facts, but values and moralities only opinions that must win out by vote or coercion.

It is disenchanted[10] in that it is a world believed to be without the binding "deep magic"[11] of a Creator who spoke the universe into a coherent symphony—and now, rather than living in a rich chorus of meaning, all is reducible to a cacophony of chemicals and accidental atoms. It is an age that has, in the words of the philosopher Roger Scruton, the nasty,

> widespread habit of declaring emergent realities to be "nothing but" the things in which we perceive them. The human person is "nothing but" the human animal; law is "nothing but" relations of social power; sexual love is "nothing but" the urge to procreation; altruism is "nothing but" the domi-

10 See Charles Taylor's *Dilemmas and Connections: Selected Essays,* ch. 12, for his treatment of "Disenchantment-Reenchantment."

11 See C. S. Lewis's essay "Talking About Bicycles" for his treatment of disenchantment. *Present Concerns* (Harcourt, 1986), 67.

nant genetic strategy described by Maynard Smith; the *Mona Lisa* is "nothing but" a spread of pigments on canvas, the Ninth Symphony is "nothing but" a sequence of pitched sounds of varying timbre.[12]

But you cannot reduce the *Mona Lisa* to brute smears of pigment and stay sane. Any lover worth being called a lover will disavow that their passion is simply the blind churning of glands and their endocrine system, nothing more. And any scientist who wishes to not be plagued by the furies of cognitive dissonance will have to work overtime to avoid thinking about how their systematic and credentialed thoughts about the world are really "just" colliding chemicals and that there is no logical reason they are to be trusted to correlate with reality at all.

2. The Age of Dis-Integration Is a *Dissociated* Age

In a world that has attempted to exorcise God from His own universe, the self is now ruptured and reality haunted. We are a bit like Voldemort (the serpentine villain of the Harry Potter series), who, in committing murder, splinters his soul, partitioning his very self in an attempt to survive whatever threats might challenge his kingdom of self.[13]

Rejecting the reality of God, we have splintered ourselves, compartmentalized our souls, and now live in a state of wide-

12 Roger Scruton, *The Soul of the World* (Princeton University Press, 2016), 39–40.

13 And yes, we are now talking about Harry Potter and horcruxes in a book about apprenticeship to Jesus.

spread dissociation—we simultaneously cling to a secularized framework while doggedly holding on to handpicked pieces of the shattered transcendent.[14] We are secular materialists when it fits our desires to make the rules we want and evade divine accountability, and yet we are also avid spiritualists when it fits our desires for there to be more to life than this.

We are those who disavow any divine authority, who renounce the ridiculous superstitions of an invisible sky-god, yet at a loved one's funeral, we are quite certain they are now "in a better place." Why? No reason but the reason of a heart shaped for eternity.

And so, it is an anxious age troubled by its unreasonable enthronement of human reason and its stubborn craving for there to be more than meaningless chemical collisions and chains of materialistic cause and effect.[15] A pervasive unease rattles in our souls as we seek signals of transcendence in a supposed Godless universe. This condition leads to a fragile sense of self prone to despair and to aggressive acts of seeking validation. That is to say, our age is an "identity crisis" factory. And

---

14 Yes, *dissociation* is a psychological term. I find it extremely helpful in understanding the ways the sin-ruptured soul tries to cope in God's world. Dissociation refers to a rupturing in how the mind processes information. Usually brought on by trauma and shame, dissociation is a coping mechanism that results in someone feeling disconnected from self and/or the world, often resulting in gaps in memory, identity confusion or alteration, and feeling as though the world is unreal (derealization).

15 This is the idea that humanity is *homo religiosus*. According to the *Encyclopedia of Psychology and Religion,* the phrase *homo religiosus* is "the idea that human existence is inherently religious. . . . [Inherent religiosity] is not a person's creedal beliefs or institutional commitments per se but refer to our existential drive toward transcendence, freedom, and meaning-making, no matter the differences of religious or a/religious backgrounds or convictions." Todd DuBose, "Homo Religiosus," *Encyclopedia of Psychology and Religion,* ed. David A. Leeming, 2nd ed. (Springer, 2014), 827–30, https://doi.org/10.1007/978-1-4614-6086-2_308.

the further into the crisis we go, the more brittle and volatile we become in constructing our identities from the heap of broken images—identities no one is allowed to question.

3. The Age of Dis-Integration Is *Discontextualized*

A cultural hurricane of excessive information has us living amid whirling bits and pieces of ologies, isms, headlines, ads, mistruths, memes, and factoids. It is not simply that things are fractured, taken out of context, and examined in isolation (*de*-contextualized), but that the pieces are *dis*-contextualized—pulled apart from their rightful place to be resituated and recombined in incongruent and nightmarish ways—and we have become normalized to such chimeras.[16] Think here of a social media feed that stitches together in "seamless flow" advertisements for hamburgers, pornographic images, silly memes, ideological rants, a friend's selfie from Disneyland, images of concrete and blood in Lebanon, and then, somewhere in the dizzying mix, a Bible verse from the book of Lamentations set between a promo for Air Jordans and an ad for Viagra. This is discontextualization. It is the de-sacralization of life.

This discontextualization is like wearing a madman's customized glasses with lenses made from shards of a thousand different prescriptions. Clarity, proportion, and scope are all lost. The rightful relationship of all things is muddled and

---

16 A chimera is a mashup sort of creature from Greek mythology that is emblematic of unnatural fusion. It usually is described as part serpent, part lion, and part goat. The term is used figuratively to mean a fanciful or impossible idea, an illusion that could not exist.

wrecked. We are being catechized by the chaos, formed by the pollution of things that ought not to be stitched together. It is Frankensteinian, and not in the Mel Brooks and Gene Wilder funny sort of way. But in the Mary Shelley *Modern Prometheus,* unnerving kind of way. Such discontextualization is the enemy of the holy—that which is sacred, that which is *set apart.*[17]

In plumbing terms, we have cross-connected the clean water and wastewater systems, not honoring (or fearing) the nature of each. We daily drink unclean water, yet we wonder why we keep getting sick. Whatever your philosophy is on life, it is an objective fact that drinking sewage will make you sick. It is an objective fact that there are things we should and should not combine. It is an objective fact that there are ways we ought not live if we want to truly live.

4. The Age of Dis-Integration Is Increasingly *Dislocated*

Digital technology has given us a gaze that far outstrips our presence. We now have anytime access to the traumas and trivialities that happen anywhere. We have far more information than proximity and power to act on the needs and opportunities, and our agency is overwhelmed in the flood of information.[18] Our souls are pulled "thin, sort of stretched,

---

17 The Hebrew word most commonly translated as "holy" is *qadosh,* and it carries the sense of someone or something being set apart, distinguished as different. Strong's Hebrew Lexicon, "qāḏôš," Blue Letter Bible, www.blueletter bible.org/lexicon/h6918/kjv/wlc/0-1.

18 In his book *Amusing Ourselves to Death,* Neil Postman calls this a low "information-action ratio."

like butter scraped over too much bread."[19] This results in the thinning of our attention and knowledge of our own moment and locale. It is not uncommon to know far more about a political coup in a distant country than what is happening in one's own city council. We are increasingly globally connected at the cost of becoming locally unrooted.

We are an increasingly asynchronous people sharing classes, conferences, and church services from different zip codes, time zones, and days of the week.[20] And I use the word *sharing* loosely. We are out of sync. Out of phase. Un-present. People and place and time are pulled apart and isolated through pervasive online engagement. And when these are pulled apart, a sense of shared story and meaning is pulled apart. We are simultaneously everywhere and nowhere. As MIT professor Sherry Turkle has written, "We are forever elsewhere."[21] And it is hard to feel the soil beneath our feet and love the person next to us when we are forever elsewhere.

5. The Age of Dis-Integration Is *Disembodied*

Our humanity is unraveling through a fistful of destructive ideologies. With the radicalizing of the inner self (the idea that ultimate authority is found in the self), we have carved up the human being. A person is not understood to be a sacred spiritual-psycho-social-physical whole, and so the body

---

19 A confession of Bilbo's from J. R. R. Tolkien's *The Fellowship of the Ring*.

20 *Asynchronous* means two or more objects or events not existing or happening at the same time.

21 Sherry Turkle, *Reclaiming Conversation: The Power of Talk in a Digital Age* (Penguin, 2015), 4.

is demoted to a loose association of bits and pieces, organic plastic that can be rearranged, removed, or replaced on a whim. In a world that is obsessed with flesh (just look at the tragic statistics regarding the porn industry), the body is rampantly commodified and devalued, used for anything and bent about in any conceivable way the autonomous self wants. Ours is an age that happily says we *have* a body to use but does not understand that we *are* embodied beings *for a sacred purpose.* The logical outcome of exiling God from the universe is that the body is no longer holy, just matter to be manipulated. We simply do not see that this body and its relationship to things and to other people is a signpost to what is most true about the world.

6. The Age of Dis-Integration Is *Disconnected*

Ironically, counter to what would be expected with the staggering advance of communication technologies and "social this" and "social that," we are an increasingly disconnected people. Statistically, loneliness and isolation are on the rise. Seventy-one percent of heavy social media users reported feelings of loneliness, up from 53 percent the year before. And 73 percent of those ages 18 to 22 (Gen Z) report sometimes or always feeling alone, up from 69 percent the year before.[22] Then there is the troubling trend of long-held family structures being dismantled, interpersonal and civic bonds eaten

---

22 Bertha Coombs, "Loneliness Is on the Rise and Younger Workers and Social Media Users Feel It Most, Cigna Survey Finds," CNBC, January 23, 2020, www.cnbc.com/2020/01/23/loneliness-is-rising-younger-workers-and-social-media-users-feel-it-most.html.

away by unchecked desires of the enthroned individual, and popularized distortions of what constitutes love and respect.

A so-called hyperconnected world has become untethered from deep interpersonal connections and attachments. Attachment bonds (deep trust connections) are intensely analog, incarnate things. Deep, healthy connections to family members are now often replaced with fickle pixelated peers and digital strangers, with tenuous promises of loyalty that will leave generations empty, suspicious, and habituated to untrust.

In sad summation, these six dis-integrating factors have uniquely coalesced in our age and have brought about what we could call the solidarity of the shattered.[23] What we share in this cultural moment is a pervasive sense of shattering and scattering—an exhausted and distracted fellowship of fragmentation.

Imagine a rock-shot windshield. There is a jagged hole at the point of impact, and radiating from that hole are multiplying fractures, branching wider as you keep speeding along. So it is with our humanity. There is a hole in the middle of our anthropology made by our break with God, and this great act of violence has compromised the integrity of it all. The cracks in the windshield of our lives keep on compounding. And as they do, it is getting harder to see where we are going through the sprawling web of fractures.

---

23 This is a play on what the Czech philosopher Jan Patočka called "the solidarity of the shaken"—a group of people who have faced a collective trauma and are ready to face its painful reality. Jan Patočka, *Heretical Essays in the Philosophy of History*, trans. Erazim Kohák (Open Court, 1996), 131.

In a God-exiled, disenchanted world, "the centre cannot hold," as the poet Yeats has warned.[24]

ANALOG MESSIAH

In this age of dis-integration, we need a coherent story that trains us in making sense of the strangeness and brilliance of the human experience. The patchwork narratives we have cobbled together about our humanity simply cannot bear the weight of our existence.

This need is what philosopher Charles Taylor spoke of as humanity's relentless *désir d'éternité:* the "desire to gather together the scattered moments of meaning into some kind of whole."[25] As I've said, the human condition aches toward integration. We long for something or someone to reverse the Babel-like confusion. There is a profound truth in the sing-song silliness of "Humpty Dumpty": He fell from a height and could not self-integrate his shattered shell of a life. Neither can we.

We need an analog Messiah. One who Himself is whole and congruent, flesh and bone and bright Spirit. A Savior who reweaves what was once divinely woven together in Eden: *place, time, and people in God's presence.* A Savior who makes it possible to say the ending is better than the beginning and worth all the mess in the middle.

---

24 William Butler Yeats, "The Second Coming," Poetry Foundation, www.poetryfoundation.org/poems/43290/the-second-coming.

25 Charles Taylor, *A Secular Age* (Belknap Press of Harvard University Press, 2007), 720.

Recall, as the story of Scripture opens, a good God creates a good world for the generative flourishing of His *very good* image bearers under His blessing. The story doesn't start with Eden riven by trauma and unraveling; it begins with God's wise weaving of the world into a tapestry of *shalom:* a thick harmony of all things working together for mutual thriving. Through the agency of His Word, God creates and orders. He forms matter. He fills with life. He shapes environs and fills them with fantastic creatures and living wonders. He sets boundaries and pairs benevolent binaries: light and dark, land and sea, night and day. He makes a land and cultivates a specific plot of it—a special place highly tuned for the flourishing of His image bearers. This is the garden of delight, or Eden.[26]

All this is done in the context of a divine cadence, a holy rhythm of days (and forthcoming seasons) marked by celestial bodies and their circuits—time. This is a physical world in sync. Properly paced. A world singing in three-part harmony.

Then God creates humanity out of the *adamah,* the soil, breathing life into the nostrils of this one He drew up from the ground.[27] God places this first human in a specific location. He is not everywhere. He is not a generic man with no place and no time. God gives the man his context, a primordial zip code. In other words, human flourishing is found in the union of place, time, and embodied presence in God's presence. When these things are separated, our very humanity

---

26 *Eden* in Hebrew is a word meaning "delight." Strong's Hebrew Lexicon, "ēden," Blue Letter Bible, www.blueletterbible.org/lexicon/h5731/kjv/wlc/0-1.

27 Strong's Hebrew Lexicon, "ădāmâ," Blue Letter Bible, www.blueletterbible.org/lexicon/h127/kjv/wlc/0-1.

is compromised. Now, with God's framework of shalom in view, the de-formative nature of digitalization begins to surface. The digital wields immense de-formative power. More so, it *encourages* the dis-integration of time, space, and embodied being as it is a form of engagement without immanent physical presence.

Apprenticeship to Jesus is intensely analog. Radically embodied. It is specific in time and place and personhood. The Christian faith is not a generality or theory. It isn't an abstraction. It isn't anonymous. It is not downloadable. It is earthy and bodily. Full of things like DNA sequences, gnarled family trees, quirky love stories, birth pains, death throes, fingerprints, and scars.

And the cure for the pervasive dis-integration of the human being is also strangely particular: Jesus, the blue-collar King from Nowhereville Nazareth, born of the virgin Mary. If this curious man whose arrival split the calendar of all history in half is truly the Son of God in human flesh, then apprenticeship to this Jesus is essential to becoming truly human. He is integral.[28] Only union with Him will unite what is riven in us. Through the agency of His Word (Jesus, the Word made flesh),[29] God is at work again weaving shalom, re-gardening the world.

In one of the most staggering passages in Scripture about the luminous identity of Jesus Christ, Paul says in Colossians 1v15–20:

---

28 *Integral* means something whole, unbroken and complete. It comes from the Latin *integer*, which means an undivided wholeness.

29 John 1v14: "And the Word became flesh and dwelt among us, and we have seen his glory, glory as of the only Son from the Father, full of grace and truth."

He is the image of the invisible God, the firstborn over all creation. For by him all things were created, in heaven and on earth, visible and invisible, whether thrones or dominions or rulers or authorities—all things were created through him and for him. And he is before all things, and in him all things hold together. And he is the head of the body, the church. He is the beginning, the firstborn from the dead, that in everything he might be preeminent. For in him all the fullness of God was pleased to dwell, and through him to reconcile to himself all things, whether on earth or in heaven, making peace by the blood of his cross.

In this Jesus Christ, "all things hold together." The Greek is *Ta panta en Christoi synesteken,* which can be translated as "All things cohere in Christ."[30] In this Jesus, the "fullness of God" dwells bodily. He is reconciling what has tragically been fractured, and He is making peace (reweaving shalom) through His sacrificial love. He is the Maker making all things right. He is the origin of all that is created, the aim for which it was always intended, and so He Himself is the way by which all things become what they were designed to be.

The unifying principle of reality is the unifying person of Jesus Christ. This one who is behind the enigmatic *strong force* that holds protons and neutrons together in their atomic dance, whose steadfast love holds our bodies and our communities together, whose wisdom holds the stars in their fiery splendor, is the very one we are called to be with and become

---

30 Joseph Henry Thayer, *Thayer's Greek-English Lexicon of the New Testament,* "sunistémi" (Hendrickson, 1996), 602.

like.[31] No wonder the Scriptures say the followers of Jesus will shine like stars.[32]

With an origin like Eden and a destiny of shining like stars, it is the most reasonable of things to be joy-haunted in the fragmented present. To long for a home to which we have not yet been. To name our ache and reach for meaning with magnificent words of longing, like *saudade, hiraeth, vemod,* and *sehnsucht.*

---

31 In the fields of nuclear and particle physics (which are way above my pay grade), the strong force is the fundamental bond that binds quarks into protons, neutrons, and other particles, weaving together the fabric of matter. It is the powerful and hidden glue that holds atoms together, making all that exists possible.

32 Daniel 12v3 says, "And those who are wise shall shine like the brightness of the sky above; and those who turn many to righteousness, like the stars forever and ever."

5

Laughing Under a Sink

Crescent Wrenches and Paradigms

There is a great market for religious experience in our world; there is little enthusiasm for the patient acquisition of virtue, little inclination to sign up for a long apprenticeship in what earlier generations of Christians called holiness.

—Eugene Peterson, *A Long Obedience in the Same Direction*

Everyone then who hears these words of mine and does them will be like a wise man who built his house on the rock.

—Jesus of Nazareth, gospel of Matthew

I found myself laughing under a sink. I was laughing because it hit me. Unexpectedly.

Some years ago, when we moved into our home near the hills and windmills of East Livermore, we did a fair amount of work on the long-neglected house, tuning it to fit our family of five. And by "tuning it" I mean gutting it and reworking it inside and out. At one point, I had installed a new cabinet and sink in the guest bathroom, and I found myself lying on my back in the small cabinet installing a chrome and porcelain double-handle faucet. That's when it hit me. Not the wrench. Not a falling faucet part. Not a spray of cold water. But the realization of what had happened to me. I had changed. I had been transformed. I had become . . . *my dad.* Or rather, *like* my dad.

In my hand was a Crescent wrench that was painted a fierce neon orange. My dad had a habit of painting his tools this bright color—it was a plumber's hack to make sure you didn't leave any tools behind in a muddy ditch or the dark corners of a crawl space. (It was a cardinal sin of our trade to leave any tool behind. One I had to repent for a number of times.) Not only was my wrench painted five-alarm orange, but it was the same brand that my father had faithfully used for decades. And there I was, holding that brilliantly orange wrench while lying under the sink just as the master plumber would. But it wasn't until I shifted position, reached up, and torqued the wrench in the same nuanced fashion I had seen the master plumber do a thousand times that I found myself laughing.

I was hundreds of miles from Colorado and my dad, and about a decade removed from being his apprentice, yet there I was, bearing an uncanny resemblance to my father, the master plumber. There I was, doing my work the way he did his, looking like him, doing what he trained me to do. There I was, *imaging* him. His ways had seeped into me, had found home in my muscle memory. The apprentice was imaging the master in a state of unconscious competence.[1]

---

1 In psychology there is a learning model called the Stages of Competence that is very relevant to the apprenticeship process as it relates to the stages of learning a skill. The four stages are (1) Unconscious Incompetence, (2) Conscious Incompetence, (3) Conscious Competence, and (4) Unconscious Competence.

But what hit me while under that sink was more than a sudden awareness of my likeness to my father. The reality of *how* apprenticeship works became clear to me. There was a simple genius and a seismic formative power to it. And it all begins with *union*. With a new relational reality.

My union with the master plumber, the relationship he called me into all those years ago—that was the beginning of my formation. There is no apprenticeship without union with a master. My new relationship with the master plumber was the source of what would follow, the new reality that would lead to reshaping me. It was a new relationship that would lead to being with the master plumber, *abiding* with him daily.

During my time as my father's apprentice, my days consisted of being with him, abiding with the master plumber on that plumbing truck and in countless crawl spaces, kitchens, and bathrooms across town. Apprenticeship is realized in the presence. In attending to one another. Apprenticeship is an inherently relational reality. Union precedes abiding, and abiding is the lived reality of that union. Transformation of a human being is always found in some orienting relationship and the formative power of its presence.

And we should be clear on this: The question is not *if* you are in some orienting and soul-forming relationship. It is *what* orienting and soul-forming relationship you are in.

But remember, apprenticeship is not simply *being united to* and then *being with*. My abiding with the master plumber was always intermingled with *obeying*. The two lived in constant dialogue. They were like breathing—the inhale and exhale of apprenticeship.

Abide—breathe in.
Obey—breathe out.
Repeat.

I was there with him not just to observe him auger a drain or install a new shutoff valve. I was there to participate. To enter into his work. I was there to absorb what he was doing into my own muscle memory, to write his likeness into the sprawling web of my neurobiology by cutting the copper and turning the wrench. After he had modeled what to do, he would put the torch in my untrained hand, and I would awkwardly solder the copper fitting, listening to his guidance from over my shoulder. And I would mess it up (he would know it before I did). I would turn on the water valve, and the joint I had just "fixed" would blow apart under the pressure. After scrambling in the spray, and when I was all wet, he would ask, "What happened?"

And then he would help me see what I couldn't see. He would have me pull the pipes apart and start again, training my perception and reflexes. I was learning to obey the master's words with my body, to listen to his way while in his presence. Learning to get his way of seeing into my eyes, to get his intuition into my gut, to wire his smooth movements into my clumsy hands. And all those years later, as I laughed under the sink with that fierce orange wrench in my hand, there I was imaging him. A reflexive imaging born of hours of labor and practice in the master's presence. I had been conformed to his image through the apprenticeship process.

But you, most likely, are not a plumber. And that's just fine, because I am not really talking about plumbing, but a fundamental truth about being human. What we need to understand is that it doesn't matter if it is plumbing in Colorado, stonemasonry in Kazakhstan, painting in Paris, farming in Lebanon, day-trading in London, or working the sous chef station at Chez Panisse just down the road from me in Berkeley; the way of apprenticeship is universal. In every context, the simple genius of apprenticeship, or what is called discipleship in the Scriptures, is:

Union → Abiding & Obeying → Imaging

As we discussed earlier, apprenticeship always begins with union. There is no apprenticeship without relationship. The union of master and apprentice is the origin of every apprenticeship. Imaging—becoming like the master—is the aim of apprenticeship. And the essence of apprenticeship that moves one from that origin of union to the aim of imaging is the way of abiding and obeying.

THE APPRENTICESHIP PARADIGM, LEO, AND JESUS

Andrea del Verrocchio. Do you know the name? Most don't. He was the master under whom Leo did his apprenticing. And by Leo, I mean of the da Vinci fame. Da Vinci became Verrocchio's apprentice when he was just fourteen years old. It was da Vinci's father who made a contract with Verrocchio that would have included mundane Renaissance apprenticeship stuff like priming wood panels and grinding paint pigments to mix with linseed oil. But what is helpful for us to see is that this relationship (union) included the fundamentals—being with Verrocchio while he worked, and listening to what

Verrocchio said when he was instructing and explaining—
abiding and obeying. This was instrumental in young da Vinci
learning how to paint like Verrocchio.

So while you may never have heard of Verrocchio, you
have seen something of who he was and how he plied his art.
For he was instrumental in shaping da Vinci, and da Vinci
shaped the *Mona Lisa,* the *Vitruvian Man, The Last Supper,*
and the *Virgin of the Rocks.* The way of the master takes on
new, embodied life in the apprentice.

It would have been something to be an apprentice to Verrocchio or to da Vinci himself—imagine the bragging rights!
Yet those who follow Jesus are apprentices of the one through
whom "all things were created," the one who is "before all
things," and in whom "all things hold together."[2] Apprentices
to the one who brought the kingdom of heaven to earth. And
so, it is crucial to see how the apprenticeship paradigm sheds
light on the way of Jesus, on what it means to be a follower of
the one who holds all things together. For the harsh reality is,
many who call themselves followers of Jesus are like those
who watch a YouTube video on sink repair and then call
themselves a plumber's apprentice. There is no reorienting relationship, no altered pattern of one's way of life—just a bit of
knowing and the attempted addressing of a particular incon-
venience. Other than that, it is life as usual.

Apprenticeship is a whole-life way of being in the world.
It cannot be compartmentalized. It is not and cannot be abstract or theoretical. It is intensely analog and presence oriented.

So, how does this apprenticeship paradigm speak specifi-

---

2 Colossians 1v16–17.

cally to following Jesus? How does the analogy of plumbing, or carpentry, or a painting apprenticeship transfer to what the Bible teaches regarding discipleship?

- **Union** with Jesus is the *origin* of apprenticeship. This grace-born miracle of a *with-God* life is given to us through the work of Jesus and ministry of His Spirit. This union with Jesus is the grace of being drawn into the triune life of God, becoming "partakers of the divine nature,"[3] that leads to re-imagining the world and re-inhabiting the world because we have been given a new nature. It all begins with union with Christ—this is what is commonly called *conversion, regeneration,* being *born anew* or *again* when the Spirit of God comes to live within us.[4]

- **Abiding** with Jesus and **obeying** Jesus are the interlaced "being and doing" of an apprentice's life—they are the renovating practices that constitute the *essence* of an embodied life of apprenticeship. Delighting in Jesus and living in accordance with what He says—this is the life-long process of transformation often called *sanctification.* This being and doing is the substance of a with-God life, empowered by the presence of God's Spirit dwelling within us. It is the life of becoming who you are,

---

3 2 Peter 1v4 speaks of the incredible truth that because of the work and in-dwelling Spirit of Jesus we have become "partakers of the divine nature" united to God in a true and nature-changing way.

4 Read John 3 to hear Jesus teach Nicodemus about being given a new nature when we are born again from above. The Greek word used for "again" is *anōthen,* which can mean both "again" (a second time) and "from above" (from heaven). Strong's Greek Lexicon, "anōthen," Blue Letter Bible, www.blueletter bible.org/lexicon/g509/kjv/tr/0-1.

working out one's "salvation with fear and trembling, for it is God who works in you, both to will and to work for his good pleasure."[5]

- **Imaging** Jesus is the *aim* of apprenticeship. The daily and ultimate purpose of our lives is to be conformed to the image of Jesus[6]—flourishing in His presence as we grow in His likeness, degree by shimmering degree. That we would be like Jesus—that is the glorious ambition of apprenticeship. This is the hope of glory we have.[7]

This paradigm is found throughout Scripture. For instance, Paul speaks about it in his letter to Titus:

For the grace of God has appeared, bringing salvation for all people, training us to renounce ungodliness and worldly passions, and to live self-controlled, upright, and godly lives in the present age, waiting for our blessed hope, the appearing of the glory of our great God and Savior Jesus Christ, who gave himself for us to redeem us from all lawlessness and to purify for himself a people for his own possession who are zealous for good works. (2v11–14)

Jesus has come to save us. Through His work of sacrificial love, through giving "himself for us to redeem us," we are united to Him (union). He is with us (abiding), as we are "a people for his own possession." He is "training us to renounce ungodliness" (obeying). And now as a people "who are zeal-

---

5 Philippians 2v12–13.

6 Romans 8v29.

7 Colossians 1v27.

ous for good works" (again, obeying), we await "our blessed hope" and His appearing, in which we will see Him face-to-face and be like Him (imaging). Throughout his writings, Paul effortlessly weaves these threads of union, abiding, obeying, and imaging into colorful tapestries of good news.

The grace that has come our way is not just the starting spark that brings about salvation, but the fuel that carries it to completion. In the apprenticeship paradigm, we see how the classic doctrines of justification, regeneration, adoption, sanctification, and glorification are interconnected.

By being united to Christ, we are *justified* (made right with God). We are *regenerated* (made alive by His Spirit, given a new nature). We are *adopted* by the Father (given the spiritual inheritance of Christ—all His blessings are now our blessings). And now having been united to Christ, we are being *sanctified*, changed. Sanctification is not self-optimization. Apprenticeship to Jesus is not white-knuckled self-improvement. Sanctification is the Spirit-empowered process of growing in Christlikeness through abiding with and obeying Jesus. And this process leads to what theologians call *glorification:* becoming mature in Christlikeness (imaging).

ANTI-APPRENTICESHIP

We often need to see the contrast of something to help us grasp what it actually is. When it comes to the apprenticeship paradigm, the de-formative inverse of it would be something like *alienation, hiding, autonomy,* and *distortion,* or:

Alienation → Hiding & Autonomy → Distortion

Here is how this de-formative process works when we are not apprenticing to Jesus. When we are not in the loving union with God that leads to flourishing, we are in a state of alienation from the One who is our very source of life. This alienation from the God who is love leads to shame (sensing that something is inherently wrong with us). Shame then leads to hiding, covering up who we truly are and suppressing who we are called to be. The shadowy partner of this life of hiding is autonomy, a hopeless kingdom of self-rule that simply cannot bring flourishing, because it turns to its finite self for nourishment rather than the dark soil, water, and bright sun of God Himself.[8] The way of hiding (shame) and autonomy (self-rule) leads to deeper and more disturbing distortions of who we are supposed to be. Rather than becoming people of increasing love and joy like the God whose image we bear, our humanity is diminished as we become more beastly, more like the serpent whose voice we are listening to. We undergo the process of spiritual de-formation, increasingly becoming misrepresentations of God.

When Jesus calls us to the way of apprenticeship, He is calling us out of the desolation of spiritual exile. He is calling us out of the shadows of hiding and into healing light. He is calling us to turn from the self-destructive way of self-reliance and self-creation. He is inviting us into the process of counter-formation, reversing the dehumanizing and deforming ways of a without-God life that have been fracturing God's good creation.

Apprenticeship doesn't arrive late on the scene somewhere in the middle or toward the end of the story. It is not a plan B

---

8 *Autonomy* is a fancy word that means "self-law." Made up from the words *auto,* meaning "self," and *nomos,* meaning "law."

when God's plan A crashed and burned. Rather, it is a first principle of reality. And its shadow, anti-apprenticeship, is there skulking in the garden too. If we can see this, it will help us to realize the absurdity of apprenticeship to Jesus being an add-on or upgrade to basic Christianity.

Apprenticeship is not simply an innovation that emerged from European feudal agricultural practices. It was not the Greeks who conceived of apprenticeship as they pondered their philosophies or carved their marble pillars. It was not someone centuries before Socrates who was whittling spears or painting on cave walls with their kids. It simply has been. And it has been since the beginning.

The essence of apprenticeship is something like gravity. It would be an odd thing to say that gravity came about in 1666 with Newton's apple incident. So too would it be strange to say apprenticeship came about with any people group or any trade. Like gravity, the way of apprenticeship was always there to be discovered, articulated, and lived out. Apprenticeship is in the bones and bloodstream of the story of human existence, an open secret hidden in plain sight.

Let's see how its origin, essence, and aim all come together in the unified narrative that unfolds through the pages of Scripture.

6

Across the Arc

Apprenticeship Along the Scriptures

"O foolish ones, and slow of heart to believe all that the prophets have spoken! Was it not necessary that the Christ should suffer these things and enter into his glory?" And beginning with Moses and all the Prophets, he interpreted to them in all the Scriptures the things concerning himself.

—Jesus of Nazareth, gospel of Luke

Other echoes
Inhabit the garden. Shall we follow?

—T. S. Eliot, *Four Quartets*

There were apprentices in Eden, you know. The way of apprenticeship is right there amid the greenery, embedded in the relational dynamics of the garden, like a 3D image camouflaged in one of those pixelated autostereogram images that proliferated in the malls of the nineties.

It would serve us well to have a biblical theology of apprenticeship. Biblical theology is not simply saying our theology (our talk about God) comes from the Bible. Rather, it is a way of reading Scripture along the arc of the narrative. It is a way of seeing the brilliant interconnectivity, the deep integration of its literary design. Sadly, it is all too common to view the Bible as something like a Norton Anthology of ancient Middle Eastern wisdom—a really old collection of writings that one can scan and flip through, plucking pearls of wisdom and advice as needed. To be clear, this is a terrible way of reading the Bible that does damage to the text and our interpretation of it.

A much healthier way of approaching the Bible is to see it as

> the God-breathed,
> humanity-penned,
> story-shaped library
> that leads us to Jesus.

This means that the Bible is God's divine self-revelation (He has shared Himself with us), written through the flesh and blood and quirks and cultural contexts of human beings (like Moses, Isaiah, and John); it is essentially a library of books consisting of various genres that are deeply cohesive and mutually interactive, pointing the thoughtful reader to Jesus. I realize there is a lot to unpack in that description. We will return to this way of understanding the Bible when we look at the practice of Scripture meditation in chapter 7, but for now we simply need to see that the Bible is an intrinsically unified story written in such a way as to not simply provide information but cultivate transformation in the reader. It is much more like Herman Melville's *Moby-Dick* than it is an encyclopedia of morality. It is far more like Dostoevsky's magisterial novel *The Brothers Karamazov* than a spiritual reference manual or a lexicon of theological terms. It is an artfully interwoven story that draws us into the heart of things, reshaping our imagination along the way.

Before I swerve off the path and go too far down the rabbit hole of the brilliant literary design of Scripture (which I am apt to do), I'll focus on the topic at hand: how the way of apprenticeship is found at the beginning, in the very heart of Eden, and how it flows from the garden throughout the vast and wild terrain of Scripture, winding its way to the glittering waters of life found in the Bible's final book, Revelation.

So let's turn our attention to the opening chapters of the book of Genesis to see union, abiding, obeying, and imaging among the flora of the Giver's good garden.

SHALOM AND SHEMA

Shalom and *shema* are two words we would do well to become acquainted with. They make for very good company when trying to make sense of apprenticeship to Jesus and how He holds all things together.[1] Likely you have heard the word *shalom*—maybe your Jewish neighbor says it in greeting, or you have heard prayers for shalom in the ever-churning news cycle regarding the turmoil in the Middle East. *Shalom* is the Hebrew word for peace—but not in the way we tend to think

---

1 Speaking of good company, I cannot talk about *shalom* and *shema* without thinking of an influential fellowship in which these things were energetically explored in class sessions, over good food, and around late-night fires. I am forever marked by the years of study and deep fellowship at Western Seminary with Gerry Breshears, Ryan Smith, Clay Worrell, Char Brodersen, Adam Dobbs, Daniel Huskey, Brad Witty, Gabriel Webb, Hakeem Bradley, Keithen Schwahn, and Crooksy.

about peace. It is not merely the absence of things going wrong. It is not simply getting along. It is a deeper reality of first things, of original good, and we should be careful not to define it by what it is not or by the derived things of the fall. Shalom is not a thin kind of peace. It is thick, multidimensional. It is the vibrant reality of all things working together for mutual flourishing. This is key for understanding how apprenticeship to Jesus is the way of flourishing in a fragmented world.

Peace isn't the fragile moment of quiet when a troubled home has a reprieve from its screaming and the emotional chaos echoing through its halls. Down the street from my childhood home was a violent house that hovers like a specter in my early memory. Its disorder not only was seen by the untended yard and beat-up façade, but was often heard by most of the neighborhood. Shalom was not the moment when the troubled house finally went quiet from all the shouting and slamming. Shalom, rather, is a well-ordered home, a love-ordered home where the mutual interdependence of family members is embodied in seeking the good of the other—where the labors of the parents are honored by a child's loving obedience; where the exhausted parent tends to their child more than nursing their own frustrations, ministering to them with a conversation, an embrace, and the last dregs of their attention. Shalom is where a spouse denies their clamoring self, lays down their rights, sees and tends to the other. Where the varied aspects of the family are not competitive but collaborative, and all the pieces fit together to better each other rather than to be better than each other. A home where each member is becoming a person of increasing love and joy. Such a web of interdependent goodness is the three-dimensional peace that is shalom. Such a peace generates life, unlike that dis-integrated home at the end of my childhood street that often bore the discolorations of abuse and the eventual news of the two boys who once lived there—news of a suicide and a prison sentence.

Again, to state the obvious, the biblical story begins on page 1 in chapter 1, not at some later point when things are unraveling. This is important because it points us to primary things, to the original and intended state God's Word spoke into existence. Out of the wild and waste of chaos, God created a good and flourishing world primed for fruitfulness. A world where all is in its place—harmony and wholeness in all directions:

- humanity in right relationship with God
- humanity in right relationship with self
- humanity in right relationship with others
- humanity in right relationship with creation

With the words "And God said," shalom was spoken into existence. The voice of God breathed the archetypal scene of things as they ought to be—a garden on a mountaintop (Eden is something of an organic temple that was the nexus, the meeting place, of heaven and earth), thriving, burgeoning with life and potential, readied for fruitfulness by way of God's presence dwelling with His people.

Okay, you may be thinking, *but what about that apprenticeship thing?*

Humanity, graciously placed into this land of shalom, received the first command, the first invitation to shema God's voice. There's that other wonderful word: *shema.* It is a Hebrew word that means much more than to merely hear sound-waves. It means "to listen" with the fullness of one's being in the context of a trusted relationship.[2] It is to listen in a way that is inseparable from love and obedience—to take in words not just with the ears, but with the heart, and to respond in trust. This means it is not just paying attention to sound, but *paying affection* to someone. As a parent, I am well acquainted with the difference between merely hearing and paying affection to the person speaking. Just because my kids hear what I say doesn't mean they shema. The words reach their ears, but not always their wills. The ears hear sounds far more readily than the heart heeds wisdom.

So, amid the shalom (all things as they ought to be), God calls His image bearers to shema (to live in accordance with what He says). And in doing so, the shalom will widen. Flourishing will fan out like light from a fire. We see this in Genesis 2v15–17:

> The LORD God took the man and put him in the garden of Eden to work it and keep it. And the LORD God commanded the man, saying, "You may surely eat of every tree of the garden, but of the tree of the knowledge of good and evil you shall not eat, for in the day that you eat of it you shall surely die."

Here is a divine call to partner with God in His grand shaloming enterprise, a partnering engaged in by hearing and obeying the Creator's Word on what is good and what is not. God has made His image bearers and blessed them, and He

---

2 *A Hebrew and English Lexicon of the Old Testament,* ed. Francis Brown, R. Driver, and Charles Briggs (Clarendon, 1906), 1033–35, "shema."

walks with them in the garden. That is union. They are in loving, trust-based relationship.

Next, we watch as man shemas (obeys) the divine voice:

> Now out of the ground the LORD God had formed every beast of the field and every bird of the heavens and brought them to the man to see what he would call them. And whatever the man called every living creature, that was its name. The man gave names to all livestock and to the birds of the heavens and to every beast of the field. But for Adam there was not found a helper fit for him. (Genesis 2v19–20)

Adam's shema-ing (trusting) is seen in this word-based work of naming the creatures (notice how it echoes the word-work of God, who created through speaking). Adam, in union with God, is abiding and obeying, which leads to him imaging his creator as he brings order about through his acts of naming/speaking. Within this compressed and compelling narrative, we see God's image bearer looking just a bit more like Him as he abides and obeys.

And this shema-ing leads to even greater shalom. Goodness will grow. How? Through the creation of the woman.

Amid his word-work of calling giraffes "giraffes" and aardvarks "aardvarks," Adam, like any good zoologist, notices the rather obvious biological reality that each of these beings comes in a set. A generative pair. There is male and female. But not for him. Adam is singular. Eve-less. There is no *other* who is both alike yet perfectly different from him. There is no equally opposite partner for a union that brings flourishing.[3]

---

3 The phrase used in Genesis 2v18 in Hebrew is *ezer kenegdo* and is often translated as "helper fit for him." A more robust translation is "like-opposite

It is at this point we hear God say it is "not good for man to be alone." This isn't just an observation that guys tend to do radically destructive things when not influenced by female presences (which is statistically true). It is an elemental truth that God wanted us to see—we are made in the image of God (who is triune, a community of love within Himself), made to know and to be known in loving community.

So let's review: Adam, in union with God his maker, has been abiding with Him and obeying Him, which has led to imaging his creator. This imaging has led to identifying something that was not so good: Adam's being alone. This revelation then leads to a new and greater shalom when God makes Eve. Adam is a *proto-apprentice*. Not because he signed up to join some gardener's guild or primeval pipe fitter's school, but simply because he was living with the grain of the universe, living with God as the organizing center of his existence. He was living in accordance with God's design by listening to His word. Loving union with God leads to abiding with Him and obeying Him—and this shema-ing way of life leads to imaging the Creator, living out His likeness here on earth. All of which leads to greater flourishing.

TWO APPRENTICES

Adam meets Eve. Which turns out to be a very good thing. So good he sings the first human song.[4] With this union of man

---

helper." *Kenegdo* is comprised of the prefix *ke* (similar/like) and the word *neged* (different). And so, wonderfully, it is a word of linked opposites that means "to complement."

4 Genesis 2v23.

and woman now in place, they can fulfill the other call to shema Him given in Genesis 1v28:

> Be fruitful and multiply and fill the earth and subdue it, and have dominion over the fish of the sea and over the birds of the heavens and over every living thing that moves on the earth.

Both man and woman, united to God and each other, are called into abiding with their Creator and invited to live in accordance with His Word. Like God, who formed and then filled the creation, His image bearers are to continue the work cultivating the raw materials of the garden (forming) and to fill the world with life. It seems the journey into a widening shalom is well on the way . . . until the next chapter.

In Genesis 3v6, we see shalom ruptured when humanity stops shema-ing God's voice and instead shemas the voice of another. Both Adam and Eve turn from God's command about not eating from the tree of the knowledge of good and evil by listening to the word of another. Eve listens to the voice of the serpent and Adam listens to the voice of Eve now echoing the serpent:

> So when the woman saw that the tree was good for food, and that it was a delight to the eyes, and that the tree was to be desired to make one wise, she took of its fruit and ate, and she also gave some to her husband who was with her, and he ate.

Adam and Eve have now shema-ed the serpent's voice rather than God's voice, which results in alienation, shame, and hiding (there's anti-apprenticeship). Turning away from God's word leads to hiding from God and each other. Beautiful unions are breaking apart. A breach has formed in the thrumming goodness of the garden.

Listening to the wrong voice fractures shalom—enmity and existential dislocation mar the wholeness and harmony of Eden. Then God comes walking in the garden. When He does, He uses His voice to initiate healing; He graciously asks a question to draw Adam and Eve out of the shadows. He will go on to tell them, "Because you have listened to the voice of your wife and have eaten of the tree of which I commanded you, 'You shall not eat of it,' cursed is the ground because of you."[5] God explicitly links the call to listen (shema), and the failure to do so, with the dis-integration of shalom. God's loving call to His image bearers was met with their creation-vandalizing response—in listening to the tempter, they became like the vandalizing serpent.

Yet all is not lost. It is also here that the seed of a promised future victory and ultimate restoration is driven into the dark soil of the garden scene. While addressing the serpent, God promises that a world-reintegrating snake crusher is on the horizon. Enter what is called the *protoevangelium* of Genesis 3v15.[6] God promises that a future descendent of Eve will someday overcome the serpent and its brood, and He will be wounded in His winning. This is a prophecy of the killing sting of the cross and the victory of the empty garden tomb of Jesus.

This pattern of shema-ing a voice other than God's and

---

5 Genesis 3v17.

6 *Protoevangelium* is the Greek term for "first gospel." *Proto* means "first" and *evangelium* means "good news."

the resultant dis-integration of shalom is found in numerous and increasingly broken iterations throughout the rest of Scripture. It is like a dark fractal fiercely spiraling through the story. For instance, in the very next chapter, Cain doesn't listen to God's voice and become more loving and life-giving like his creator; instead, he follows the voice of temptation into the murdering of his brother Abel, and therefore becomes more like the serpent who comes to steal, kill, and destroy. Cain *images* the invading serpent rather than the garden maker. Sin is like a beast crouching at his door, ready to pounce[7]—and in listening to the tempter's voice, Cain becomes like a crouching beast, a coiled serpent that strikes his own brother. This disunion from God, this alienation, leads to Cain's exile to the east, a life of autonomy, and a family line that progressively distorts God's image here on earth. Cain has apprenticed under the serpent, and his way of life will twist and gnarl a family tree.

Now, fast-forward to the time of Abram and Sarai.[8] God calls Abram out of Eden's exile in the east, out of a bustling metropolis called Ur, and tells him to head west. Abram obeys and inches the story forward toward a restoring of shalom. Abram's abiding with God and obeying God will lead to his being an agent of worldwide flourishing, like his God. That's *imaging*. God promises that all the world will be blessed through Abram's forthcoming star-field of a family.[9] But in the mix of it all, doubting God's promise of a child to their aging bodies, Sarai *offers* to Abram the *taking* of Hagar to claim the

---

7 Genesis 4v6–7.
8 Genesis 11 and 12.
9 Genesis 15v5–6.

promised child by their own means. They objectify and abuse an image bearer to obtain a promise of God. Genesis 16v2 culminates in the resonant sentence "And Abram *listened* to the *voice* of Sarai." Sarai and Abram trusted a narrative other than God's, and it sent fractures sprawling through the family that are still shedding blood today in the Middle East. Anti-apprenticeship shows up, and it brings about generations of family alienation, hiding, autonomy, and dehumanizing distortion. This should evoke narrative déjà vu, as this is an iteration of Genesis 3: Hagar is *seen* as a good solution, *taken,* and *given* like the fruit of the tree, and Abram, like Adam and Eve, listens to the tempter's voice (now heard in the words of Sarai). It's the old story remixed.

The same pattern is found later in Genesis 27 when Rebekah tells her son Jacob to "obey my voice." She then *takes* the tools of deception (goats from the flock and musky clothes from Esau's hunting closet) and *gives* misleading food (like Eden's fruit) to Jacob so that he might trick his father and steal his brother's inheritance. Here, in the garden of this dysfunctional family, Rebekah takes on the serpent's role in offering an alternative narrative to God's promise as she plies the work of deception. It is yet another replay, another variant of Genesis 3.

The shema pattern also shows up in the story of Joseph (the one with the amazing technicolor dreamcoat). Joseph, who listens to God's voice, is thrown in a pit, taken into slavery, and ends up in an Egyptian prison. However, Joseph's refusal to heed the anti-God voices in his life leads to a redemptive suffering from which new life emerges. Joseph's abiding with God and obedience to God's word leads to this "beloved son of Israel" rising from the pit of death and becoming a hero as his actions eventually bring bread to a world rocked by famine. He has become more like his creator, imaging Him in bringing shalom to chaos, forgiving his murderous brothers, and bringing reconciliation. Yet, the newfound life for Jew and Gentile that comes through Joseph is ultimately not enough to truly reweave shalom—for the book of Genesis ends with breathless old bones in a coffin. This should not surprise us; a corpse in a gutted tree is the supreme icon for the shattered shalom of Eden.[10]

This is not the way it is supposed to be, and these destructive movements of not shema-ing the voice of God will resound throughout the Scriptures in increased frequency and amplitude.

APPRENTICES IN THE WILDERNESS

Over time, Joseph's descendants multiply in the land of Egypt in a garden-like region called Goshen. Years pass, a new pharaoh rises to replay the destructive role of the serpent, and God's people are enslaved. Then God raises up Moses to be an agent of redemption. He sends this reluctant shepherd to the unnamed pharaoh of Exodus with words for him to shema: "Let my people go!" Words the pharaoh hears but doesn't heed—it is a disobedience to love that will lead to the death of his firstborn son and countless others.

Eventually, God gives Moses instructions about what will become known to the Jewish people as *Pesach,* or Passover. A

---

10 Genesis 50v26. The meditative reader will see here not only a poignant link back to the garden but also a shadow of a future son of Abraham dead upon a tree. Here as Genesis ends, we are given a subtle clue about how humanity's exile from Eden will ultimately be reversed—a rejected savior like Joseph will one day die on a tree of life.

death is coming to the land of oppression and tyranny that will lead to a new life of freedom for God's people. Every household, Jew and Gentile, will know the death of a firstborn unless they obey what God has spoken to them through Moses. The blood of a young, unblemished lamb must be shed and painted on their doorframes. For those who listen to these strange instructions, death passes over their home and the passage to freedom opens before them. This act of trust in God's peculiar word about lamb's blood on wooden beams brings flourishing. The people are finding the way to life through apprenticeship to this God who is working on their behalf. God is working to unite a people to Himself—a people who will dwell with Him, obey Him, and become like Him.

Again, scroll forward along the time bar of the story to when God's people have left Egypt and are now on the other side of the divided Red Sea. No sooner has God proven that trust in Him leads to life than the newly freed people mistrust Him and accuse Him of *not being good.* The people grumble and groan in the wilderness, accusing God of trying to kill them. They have listened to the tempter's voice and become his mouthpiece, echoing the serpent's tactic in Genesis 3 of questioning the goodness of a good God.

In a painfully brief summation of the wilderness years written about in Exodus, Leviticus, and Numbers, when the people abide with and obey the God who brought them into relationship with Himself, they become more and more like Him, agents of love and flourishing; when they alienate themselves from His love, refusing to obey His words of life, they become dehumanized and distorted. The wilderness is a school of apprenticeship to the God who made us in His image.

THE SECOND WORD

Now to Deuteronomy, the last book of the Torah. *Deuteronomy* means "second law." It is called that because here God again speaks His words of life to bring flourishing to His people, reiterating what was said at Sinai. After some forty years of wandering in the wilderness, the people of Israel are now crouched (yes, that is an allusion to Cain's story) on the edge of the promised land. Here on the threshold to the garden-like land of milk and honey, Moses speaks of God's call to shema His voice and recounts the innumerable shalom-vandalizing actions of Israel's past: *Remember how God has been faithful and how you have been unfaithful to Him!* It is here that we encounter the extremely important passage of Deuteronomy 6v4–6 known as the Shema. The essence of the Shema is a call to listen and obey through a loving trust in God who has revealed Himself to humanity:

> Hear, O Israel: The LORD our God, the LORD is one. You shall love the LORD your God with all your heart and with all your soul and with all your might. And these words that I command you today shall be on your heart.

At the conclusion of his speech, Moses gives a warning and ultimatum. To shema God will lead to blessing, but to disobey will perpetuate the shattering of shalom, eventually leading to the nation's exile (another iteration of the crucial choice at the center of Eden with the tree of life and the tree of the knowledge of good and evil). Moses knows that exile is on the distant horizon for God's people. Yet even so, Moses looked forward to a day when God would give Israel a *hearing heart* that they may truly live.

Then, as the Torah (the five books of Moses) closes, the reader gets gut-punched: Moses is locked outside of that promised land because of his own failure to shema God's word.[11] It's heartbreaking. Moses, too, had failed to listen to God. After all the miles traveled, and now in sight of the promised land, Moses faces death just outside the finish line. Really? What does this mean? The Torah ends with a heavy-hearted declaration that, though Moses was a towering figure in the history of redemption, he was not the promised shalom-bringer spoken of in Genesis 3v15. He, too, fell short. Moses didn't shema the command of God to speak to the rock.[12] Instead of heeding God's life-bringing voice to call forth water, he struck the rock, taking matters into his own hands. He judged for himself what was right to do. He failed to listen by failing to speak as God commanded. Moses was not God's perfect agent of the divine Word. This perfect agent of the divine Word won't come for well over a millennium until the birth of the one of whom the apostle John writes, "The Word became flesh and dwelt among us, and we have seen his glory, glory as of the only Son from the Father."[13]

The Torah ends with a call to shema and an amplified ache for God to bring shalom: "Moses was 120 years old when he died. His eye was undimmed, and his vigor unabated. And the people of Israel wept for Moses in the plains of Moab thirty days."[14] And then, in a foreshadowing plea to the reader,

---

11 Numbers 20v12.

12 Numbers 20v7–11.

13 John 1v14.

14 Deuteronomy 34v7–8.

an editorial comment links what has happened with the next book of Scripture:

> Joshua the son of Nun was full of the spirit of wisdom, for Moses had laid his hands on him. So the people of Israel obeyed him and did as the LORD had commanded Moses. And there has not arisen a prophet since in Israel like Moses, whom the LORD knew face to face, none like him for all the signs and the wonders that the LORD sent him to do in the land of Egypt, to Pharaoh and to all his servants and to all his land, and for all the mighty power and all the great deeds of terror that Moses did in the sight of all Israel.[15]

A greater prophet was needed. A greater rescuer was required. Moses was marvelous and epic, but he was not *the* promised serpent crusher of Genesis 3v15. Maybe the next leader would be the promised one? Maybe it would be this stellar fellow named Joshua? He seems to have a lot of potential. His very name refers to salvation.[16]

This Joshua is presented as not only a new Moses but a new Adam called to reclaim and guard the promised land (like Eden). How is he to do this? Here again the Eden-creating voice is to be listened to:

> This Book of the Law shall not depart from your mouth, but you shall meditate on it day and night, so that you may be careful to do according to all that is written in it. For then

---

15 Deuteronomy 34v9–12.

16 The name Joshua comes from the Hebrew name Yehoshua, which means "Yahweh is salvation" or "The LORD saves." The name Joshua (Yehoshua) is the same name that becomes *iēsous* in Greek and Jesus in English.

you will make your way prosperous, and then you will have
good success. Have I not commanded you? Be strong and
courageous. Do not be frightened, and do not be dismayed,
for the LORD your God is with you wherever you go.[17]

God's word and God's presence are explicitly linked with
the people's flourishing.

Abiding with and obeying this God is what leads to life.
This Joshua is not just an apprentice of Moses; he is to be an
apprentice of God.

At this point in the story, God's voice of "Let there be" and
"It is good" from Genesis 1 takes the form of the "book of the
Law"—the Torah. How is Joshua to pursue his Adam-like
calling? How is he to walk with YHWH? He is to do it by
listening to the voice of YHWH through His self-revelation
given in the Torah. If Joshua meditates on it, repeats it, eats
and breathes it, shemas it, he will be an agent of shalom-
making in the renewal of Eden; he will be a blessed partner in
God's good plan and dwell in His life-giving presence.

We should notice in the passage that meditation is linked
to doing, abiding linked to obeying: "Be careful to do according to all that is written."[18] Success here is defined by shema-
ing the Word of God. By the time the book of Joshua comes
to a close, Joshua has shown a stellar track record in regard to
listening to God's voice. Under his administration, it seems
that shalom is ascending and the people are meditating on
God's Word and serving the Lord.[19] But the book's closing
ends with another burial. And not only that, but a grave re-

---

17 Joshua 1v8–9.
18 Joshua 1v8.
19 Joshua 24v31.

minder of Joseph's bones having been carried from Egypt and buried in Shechem[20]—which serves to reload the present story with the reverberating traumas of slavery, family dysfunction, and the distorting of the covenant symbol in the bloodshed at Shechem. And then, for the third stroke against shalom, the story tells us that "Eleazar the son of Aaron died." Not only does Moses's successor die, but the son of the priest dies too. The point? Restoration of Eden is still on the far horizon. "Keep looking," the Scriptures say. "We are not there yet. There are miles to go until peace."

We have just barely dipped our imaginations into the patterns of apprenticeship along the arc of the story. I haven't even spoken here of King David or the Psalms, the apprenticeship-rich lives of Elijah and Elisha, or the electric writings of the prophets. As one thoughtfully traces the storyline of Scripture, in book after book, we see the apprenticeship paradigm (and its collapse) in operation. We see people lovingly trust in God and taste flourishing. We see God's people fail to dwell with and obey a good God who has acted on their behalf— and so fall into the dis-integration of death. We see signpost after desperate signpost that only God can re-garden the dis-integrated world. Only the Word made flesh can bring true shalom. Only the ultimate Adam (Jesus), and the bride born from His side (the church), can bring shalom to a fragmented world.

Moses could not un-grumble the hearts of the people. Joshua could not destroy the deep-seated structure of sin in the human condition. King David in all his warrior-poet awe-

---

20 Shechem is a location in which a number of violent acts mar Israel's family history.

someness could not be the perfect shepherd-king. Solomon's wisdom gave way to folly. Elijah and Elisha, for all their wonderworking and blistering warnings, could not save a kingdom in a downward spiral of sin. A hero must arrive on the scene, from within both the human family and deep heaven itself, who has the power to turn hearts of stone to flesh. One who can unite a fractured people to Himself and empower them with a new nature to abide with and obey Him. One who can take dehumanized and splintered image bearers and transform them from one degree of glory to another, forming them into whole and holy human beings. And so, the Old Testament ends with an aching ellipsis, a yearning, "to be continued . . ."

Then Jesus steps onto the dis-integrated scene and says to broken hearts, *Lech acharai—Come, follow Me.*

Follow Me into the wholeness of holiness. Become My apprentice in love and joy.

PART TWO
Re-Inhabiting
a Fragmented World

. . . until Christ is formed in you.

—Paul, letter to the Galatians

Let us begin with practices, overt behavior. Spiritual formation *in Christ* is oriented toward explicit obedience to
Christ. The language of the Great Commission, in Matthew
28, makes it clear that our aim, our job description as
Christ's people, is to bring *disciples* to the point of obedience
to "all things whatsoever that I have commanded you." . . .
Of course, this assumes that we ourselves are in obedience,
having learned *how* to obey Christ. Though the inner dynamics are those of love for Christ, he left no doubt that the
result would be the keeping of his commandments.

—Dallas Willard, *The Great Omission*

My Dear Wormwood,

I note with grave displeasure that your patient has become a Christian. . . . There is no need to despair; hundreds
of these adult converts have been reclaimed after a brief so-
journ in the Enemy's camp and are now with us. All the
habits of the patient, both mental and bodily, are still in our
favor.

—C. S. Lewis, *The Screwtape Letters*

7

Scripture Meditation

Listening to God's Word
Above All Other Voices

If you feel that we live in a purely physical universe, you will view meditation as a good way to obtain a consistent alpha brain-wave pattern. But if you believe that we live in a universe created by the infinite-personal God who delights in our communion with him, you will see meditation as communication between the Lover and the beloved.

—Richard Foster, *Celebration of Discipline*

A story is a way to say something that can't be said any other way, and it takes every word in the story to say what the meaning is. You tell a story because a statement would be inadequate. When anybody asks what a story is about, the only proper thing is to tell him to read the story.

—Flannery O'Connor, *Mystery and Manners*

Over time, it became mostly duct tape. The pocket-sized Bible no longer sported its burnished cover. It was now bound in the functional gray and string-lined texture of duct tape.

This re-skinning had not happened all at once, though.

Over years of being carried in the back left pocket of my Carhartts, pored over in the spaces between service calls, handled with rough hands, read by flashlight in cobwebbed vaults and crawl spaces, and smudged with sweat and lunch oils, the cover wore thin and fell to pieces. So, as one does when on a plumbing truck with a deteriorating Bible in their hands, I reached for the duct tape and added layer after layer to keep it together. There's a popular myth that every seven years the human body is made up of entirely different cells, utterly reconstituted through cellular death and regeneration. I don't know about that, but it did take just a few years of long blue-collar days to reconstitute a Bible cover with duct tape.

One day I was holding those duct tape–bound pages when someone asked, "When are you going to get your head out of that book and start doing something practical with your life?" Which, in my opinion, was a rather curious thing to say. First, because I was holding it while working as a service plumber, which seems a very practical thing given the urgency with which people want their toilets fixed and hot water turned back on. Second, the only thing more practical than having your head in the Bible is having the Bible in your head. There is nothing more practical for living in accordance with reality than having one's imagination reshaped by the story God tells about who He is and who we are and what all this is for. And that brings us to the practice of *Scripture meditation*.

Apprentices of Jesus are a people who practice Scripture meditation: listening to the Word of God above all other voices.

HONEY ON A CHALKBOARD

Honey to dust. In the days of Jesus, apprenticeship would begin with the sweetness of honey on the tongue and would lead to the strange glory of being covered in a rabbi's dust.[1]

At the age of five or six, the child would begin their formal education. Entering into our equivalent of elementary school, a Jewish child would enter *Bet Sefer*—House of the Book. On the first day of class, these young students were handed a chalkboard, a piece of slate, with the Hebrew alphabet and some verses of the Torah written on it. These fledgling students would then be led by their teacher in repeating aloud the alphabet and passages—and then honey would be dripped onto their chalky slates. To the young students' delight, they were to lick the sticky slate and their honeyed fingers. Standards of cleanliness aside, it is not hard to imagine the widening eyes of six-year-olds at the oozing of golden honey down their gray slates. Seems a rather brilliant way to start a school year and begin to retrain one's hungers and habits.

The drizzle of honey along the words of God—here, at the very start of their formation, is a visceral object lesson in the sweetness of the Torah, in the goodness of God's Word, which they would learn to feast upon, to savor and take into their inner being that it might change them from the inside out. The very idea of "Word as honey" and "Word as way" comes from Psalm 119v103–105:

---

1 Pirkei Avot 1:4, in *The Mishnah,* trans. Herbert Danby (Oxford University Press, 1933), 446. "Let thy house be a meeting-house for the Sages and sit amid the dust of their feet and drink in their words with thirst."

How sweet are your words to my taste,
    sweeter than honey to my mouth!
Through your precepts I get understanding;
    therefore I hate every false way.
Your word is a lamp to my feet
    and a light to my path.

Honey on a chalkboard: a fitting image of Scripture meditation that links the goodness of God with the formative power of practice.

PRACTICES OF GRACE

Apprenticeship to Jesus begins with union with Jesus by His Spirit—that's the *origin*. In this glad union we are justified, regenerated, and adopted. Apprenticeship to Jesus will ultimately lead to imaging Him, which is the great *aim*. And what is the way from union to imaging? The path from the origin to the aim of apprenticeship is *abiding* and *obeying*. The *essence* of apprenticeship is a life of obedient abiding, which is done through the practices of grace. These practices of grace are how we inhabit the world—the ways in which our hungers and habits are trained to delight in and orient our lives to God. They are the things we do that do things to us.[2] They are practiced wisdom that trains us in godliness, rewriting our old, twisted neural pathways that sin has etched in us, reworking our old muscle memories to become new loving ones.

---

2 James K. A. Smith has wittily written, "These aren't just things we do; they do something to us," in *You Are What You Love: The Spiritual Power of Habit* (Brazos, 2016), 38.

Before we look deeper into this first and foundational practice of Scripture meditation, let me be abundantly clear: The practices are not means of earning salvation or making God love us. But they most certainly are works resulting from being saved by grace. They are actions born of the Spirit, evidence of the new life we have through union with Jesus. Again, one of the symptoms of the age of dis-integration is pitting good things against each other that should live in harmony. It is not "salvation by grace through faith" *or* "a life of good works" any more than respiration is only either breathing in or breathing out.

The practices are not simply *trying*. They are Spirit-empowered *training*.[3] They are training in becoming people of love and joy, like Jesus. They are everyday acts of trust in God that form us, that make what is currently impossible possible. They are grace-empowered effort in the process of working out our salvation with fear and trembling.[4]

I love the haunting sound of the cello. However, if on some Monday morning my desire to play the cello moved me to do so, I could not simply pick up the instrument and play it out of raw desire. I have never learned to play the cello. All the desire in the world to make that thing sing in that moment would only produce some painful squeaks and screeches. For that cello to sing like it was designed, I would have to tune my knowing, my muscles, my nervous system with practice. The abstractions of scales and melodies would have to be written into my body. I would need training to play something beautiful.

---

3 Philosopher and author Dallas Willard is a Jedi in helping to understand the difference between trying and training.

4 Philippians 2v12.

In other words, training allows us to do things we could not do directly (this is called indirection), even though we have a desire to do that thing. As apprentices of Jesus who have His Spirit within us, we have desires that are being graciously reshaped and redirected so that we may live in increasingly loving ways. This is happening while our old muscle memories of sin are still hard at work, rebelling and reflexively doing the things we have long done but no longer want to do. This war of desire that Paul calls "the flesh" (habituations of sin within us) is not evidence of a lack of apprenticeship. Rather, it is evidence that we are following a new Master and learning how to truly live—just as fumbling fingers on a cello's fingerboard are evidence of learning how to play.

What is needed is a life of obedience that serves to bring the body along with the holy desires granted us by the indwelling presence of the Spirit. As apprentices, we are being trained to re-inhabit reality in the way of Jesus. This is a lifelong, joyful, and often painful training process called *progressive sanctification*. It is learning to live by dying to the ways we used to be. It is learning to taste and see that God is good.

Now, back to honey and dust.

LISTENING TO GOD'S WORD
ABOVE ALL OTHER VOICES

The practice of Scripture meditation is fundamental to re-inhabiting a fragmented world.

Scripture meditation is listening to God's Word above all other voices.

Every day, we wake up and are confronted with the choice of what voice we will listen to. What narrative about reality will we say yes to? Will we listen to the de-forming narratives about what success is, or what love is, or what marriage is, or what gender is, brought to us through the well-honed story-telling and potent cinematography of our latest Netflix binge? Will we allow the culmination of curated images we scroll past daily to unconsciously shape our ideas of justice, politics, and sexuality more than the teachings of Jesus?

The narratives, the stories we meditate on, are shaping our imaginations about what is real. Myriad voices are hard at work bending us, fueling destructive desires, cultivating appetites, normalizing and valorizing things that once seemed impossible in culture.

In a shalom-shattered world, we need the shalom-bringing Word of God to counter-form us, to help retrain our desires toward what is loving and true. We need to see and to be with Jesus—by way of His Word. We are to, in the words of the Word itself, "let the word of Christ dwell in [us] richly" and to "not be conformed to this world, but be transformed by the renewal of [our] mind."[5]

Life in God's world is always call-and-response. God has *spoken*. God *is*. God is *first* and *primary*, and we as His creatures, as His image bearers, are to *respond* in trust to His Word that is only and always true. This is why faith is a matter of life and death: To trust God is to go the way of flourishing; to not trust Him, but to listen to a counter-narrative, another voice, is to go the way of perishing.

This is what Psalm 1 is all about—two ways of being in the

---

5 Colossians 3v16 and Romans 12v2.

world: flourishing and perishing. God's Word is the fulcrum between the two. According to the psalmist, the wise person doesn't listen to the words, the counsel, or the way of the wicked. The wise person is wise precisely because they shema the Word of God.

Psalm 1

Blessed is the man
    who walks not in the counsel of the wicked,
nor stands in the way of sinners,
    nor sits in the seat of scoffers;
but his delight is in the law of the LORD,
    and on his law he meditates day and night.

He is like a tree
    planted by streams of water
that yields its fruit in its season,
    and its leaf does not wither.
In all that he does, he prospers.
The wicked are not so,
    but are like chaff that the wind drives away.

Therefore the wicked will not stand in the judgment,
    nor sinners in the congregation of the righteous;
for the LORD knows the way of the righteous,
    but the way of the wicked will perish.

The psalmist is teaching us vital things here at the start of the book of Psalms—which is filled with lessons on how to live a with-God life. It is a trade school of trust made up of

150 classes of learning how to abide and obey.[6] Here we learn that the Scriptures are *meditation* literature, not *microwave* literature. We live in a cultural moment that wants to microwave everything. Immediacy has become an unquestioned, culture-controlling virtue. ChatGPT gives us instant answers for anything. Digital music services grant us immediate access to any song we want, granted we pay the subscription fees. Worldwide feedback happens in a flash with likes and comments validating or blasting our latest social media post. In the blurred hurry of it all, we have confused whirling hurricanes of information for the rhythmic breath of wisdom. But the reality remains: You can't microwave an acorn into an oak tree. It must be planted in humble soil and, through countless seasons, must soak in the water and take in the light. Only then will the life within transform into the trunk and branches of a towering tree.

I should point out here that there is a big difference between Eastern meditation and the type of meditation spoken of in Psalm 1. Unfortunately, the word *meditation* can make some of us a bit twitchy. Scripture meditation is not an emptying of one's mind and simply looking within the depths of the self for wisdom. Rather, it is the filling of one's mind with God's Word, looking to Him who is looking to you in love—a life-giving love that makes us new.

This type of meditation has a content (what God has spoken), yet it is concerned about our formation, not merely information transmission. It is not sheer data acquisition, like silicon servers can do. It is a soul thing, as it has to do with all

---

6 The book of Psalms contains 150 psalms. These songs are divided into five sections that echo the five books of the Torah (Genesis, Exodus, Leviticus, Numbers, and Deuteronomy).

of who we are. Meditation on God's Word is *unrushed reflection for deep transformation.* Think of it as feasting on God's Word to get what is beautiful, good, and true deep into the fibers of our being, our imagination, and our muscle memory.

HAGAH

The psalmist says we are to *hagah* God's Word—the Hebrew word *hagah* is translated as "meditate." It is a savory word with great resonance. It means something closer to "mutter, speak, or growl" rather than merely "to think upon." Hagah is an onomatopoeia—it sounds like what it is.[7] Its two breathy and guttural syllables evoke the sound of a lion gnawing on its prey, jawing on the meat and bones of its Serengeti lunch. As it gnaws on its feast, it purrs, growls, sighs. Hagah is the sound of unhurried savoring.

When you eat that filet mignon you love, first you go to the effort of getting it. Somehow it is on your plate. Then, bite by bite, you put it in your mouth. Chew it. Swallow it. Your digestive system churns it. It is assimilated into the very tissues of your being as you metabolize it. It changes you at the cellular level. Because of it, you are physiologically altered from the inside out. The death that is that filet mignon is now life to you, energizing you. This rather strange act of taking something *other* into your own being enables you to live and to move and to be. To go on a long walk. To pull weeds in the garden. To fix a sink. To play games with your kids.

---

7 Try saying it aloud over and over to get the effect: "Hagah, hagah, hagah . . ." Strong's Hebrew Lexicon, "hāḡâ," Blue Letter Bible, www.blueletterbible.org /lexicon/h1897/kjv/wlc/0-1.

Hagah-ing is transformative. It is an act we do directly that leads to something wonderful that we cannot do directly. We cannot manifest nutrition and energy through sheer will-power. Rather, we hagah—we take in, bite by bite—that life from without that will work to change us from within. This is the Hebrew understanding of meditation: an eating of, a delighting in, an unhurried, effort-engaged intensive and focused reading of God's Word. A feasting on divine love. The life within is dependent upon life from without.

Scripture meditation is unhurried, repetitive, and recursive.[8] It repeats and rehearses things, turning the biblical texts like a gemstone in light to watch them catch fire from different angles. It returns to what has been read before, discovering how it is interconnected and mutually illuminating with other scriptures. As silence is undone with sound, Scripture meditation is undone with hurry. We are not to rush to grab an easy answer, to strip-mine the terrain of text for some useful data and move on to something new (which is a chronic disease of our day and age). Novelty addiction is an enemy of wisdom.

Just as our body needs food and water, our inner person needs to feed on the truth and love of God's self-revelation. It really is as Jesus said to Satan when He was in the wilderness, hungry and tired: "Man shall not live by bread alone, but by every word that comes from the mouth of God."[9] That was no Christianese answer. It was a declaration of the soul's deepest need—intimacy with the God who has spoken us into being and spoken to us as His beloved.

---

8 Something that's recursive is looped, especially in a way that allows a process to keep repeating or referring back to something.

9 Matthew 4v4.

This is what Psalm 1 is teaching with the image of the tree. As the tree dwells in the soil by the stream, constantly supplied with life-giving water, it grows slowly. Matures quietly. Is stabilized as its roots dig deep into the earth's darkness. Gently, gradually, it becomes generative, bearing fruit in season. It matures as it weathers the wilds of the seasons—the pleasant days, pressing winds, and once-in-a-century storms all become incorporated into its identity.

So, too, will apprentices of Jesus slowly grow in love, joy, peace, hope, resilience, and fruitfulness as they drink up the life-giving Word of God through a lifetime of Scripture meditation. This is why Paul tells us in Philippians 4v8–9:

> Finally, brothers, whatever is true, whatever is honorable, whatever is just, whatever is pure, whatever is lovely, whatever is commendable, if there is any excellence, if there is anything worthy of praise, think about these things. What you have learned and received and heard and seen in me— practice these things, and the God of peace will be with you.

Scripture meditation takes time and attention. It cannot be delegated to another. Though it can be bolstered by others, it cannot be relinquished to a pastor or outsourced to some sermon clip online. It cannot happen at warp speed or at doomscrolling speed. It is a countercultural practice that happens at a countercultural speed—the pace of patient intimacy. It is no secret that the dominating cultural architectures of Western society are actively opposed to such deep, unrushed, reflective reading. We are busy with other things. We inhale torrents of media. We scroll at blurring speeds. The attention economy is ravenous for our time and energies, and it is relentlessly consuming us as we consume its products.

As we browse website after website, scroll news feed after news feed, our reading experience is *uncultivated* to be shallow and swift. Our age of digital distraction is keenly engineered to maximize addiction. Calculated bursts of images and information release a rush of dopamine in our brains—a neurotransmitter that ignites desire. But these relentless rushes of dopamine don't serve to satisfy us. They hollow us out with the hyperactive need for more—more input, more stimulation, more hits of "the new." Again, these overactive dopamine bursts are the neurological equivalent of drinking salt water.

WHAT WE FEAST UPON

What is it we feast upon when we hagah the Scriptures?

> The Bible is
> the God-breathed,
> humanity-penned,
> story-shaped library
> that leads us to Jesus.

The Scriptures are God-breathed and humanity-penned. Of heaven, yet earthy. In 2 Timothy 3v14–17, Paul writes to his protégé, Timothy, about the double nature of Scripture:

> As for you, continue in what you have learned and have firmly believed, knowing from whom you learned it and

how from childhood you have been acquainted with the sacred writings, which are able to make you wise for salvation
through faith in Christ Jesus. All Scripture is breathed out
by God and profitable for teaching, for reproof, for correc-
tion, and for training in righteousness, that the man of God
may be complete, equipped for every good work.

Paul calls Scripture *theopneustos:* God-breathed. God's
Spirit has fashioned it. Brought it forth. Inspired it. *In-spired:*
breathed into being. It is not the invention of human beings
who are pondering religious things. It is God's divine self-
expression penned through the agency of His image bearers.

Peter speaks of this God-breathed nature as well in 2 Peter
1v19–21:

We have the prophetic word more fully confirmed, to which
you will do well to pay attention as to a lamp shining in a
dark place, until the day dawns and the morning star rises in
your hearts, knowing this first of all, that no prophecy of
Scripture comes from someone's own interpretation. For no
prophecy was ever produced by the will of man, but men
spoke from God as they were carried along [*pheromenoi*] by
the Holy Spirit.

That Greek word for carried along, *pheromenoi,* means
to do the work of moving something from here to there.[10]
The gospel author Luke uses the term for a storm's wind
that moves a ship across the Mediterranean Sea.[11] The Spirit

---

10 Strong's Greek Lexicon, "pherō," Blue Letter Bible, www.blueletterbible
.org/lexicon/g5342/kjv/tr/0-1.

11 Acts 27v15.

has done the moving from *here to there*—done the work of bringing the Word of God to humanity. And He has done it through human agents—similar to how a wind moves a boat along through the instrument of its sails. Scripture is humanity-penned, meaning that God spoke through His image bearers. It did not appear out of thin air. It did not fall out of the sky like a sacred meteorite. Scripture has come to us through hands on papyrus, through reed pens, lamp-black ink, and particular personalities hovering over pages of human language.

God's Word, like Jesus, is both divine and human. The written Word of God and the Word made flesh are miraculously similar in this both-and way. The Bible is also plural and singular. Plural in books, singular in that it is story-shaped, having a unified narrative. The word *Bible* comes from the Greek word *biblia,* which means "books." Plural. God's written Word is a book of books. A library of books. Sixty-six books, to be exact.

Consisting of a variety of genres, the Bible is roughly 43 percent narrative, 33 percent poetry, and 24 percent prose discourse.[12] This means that we have to be conscious of what we are reading and to be agile in relationship with it. It means God is fond of story and finds it helpful for us to grow in love. It also means God must think poetry valuable and that it has much to do with theology (which would be good for us to consider in a world that sidelines poetry in favor of pragmatism and efficiency). It also means we are to read the Bible literarily, attentive to genre. Notice I said *literarily,* which is different from literally but includes *literally* in its reading

12 "Literary Styles," *How to Read the Bible* series, BibleProject, June 22, 2017, https://bibleproject.com/explore/video/literary-styles-bible.

toolbelt. Just because something is symbolic does not mean
it is not true. Just because something is true does not mean it
cannot be portrayed with symbol. In other words, we are to
be pondering the nuanced artistry and meaning-laden structures of the text. The book of Acts is to be read differently
than the book of Revelation. Both are true. Yet they function differently—Acts is a history; Revelation is apocalyptic
literature. The Bible is true in the truest sense, and it is true
through its genres.

This genre-rich library is story-shaped, meaning it is radically cohesive and has a plot. Its sixty-six books were written
by more than forty authors over the course of fifteen hundred
years. It weaves through ten civilizations, across three conti-
nents, and is written in three languages. Through all those
ages, authors, languages, and cultures, the pieces work together, telling the unified story of the God who is ultimately
revealed in Jesus Christ. The deeper one excavates, the more
coherent the Scriptures are found to be. That's something to
reckon with.

It is not a hodgepodge of parables, principles, and dis-
jointed stories. It is a story of stories. There is a narrative arc
of promise and tension that runs from Genesis to Revelation.
Genesis is full of seeds that germinate, grow, blossom, and
bear fruit in the branches of the other books. The things Jesus
says and does don't materialize from thin air; they are thickly
rooted in the fertilized soil of Israel's history. The unfurled
wonders of the New Testament are coiled in the DNA of the
Torah. A quick consideration of the book of Revelation shows
that it weaves hundreds of scriptural themes, patterns, shadows, and fulfillments into a single, remarkably unified conclusion to the Bible.

And all its hyperlinked brilliance leads to encountering Jesus.

In the gospel of John, Jesus addresses the misappropriation of Scripture with these staggering words:

> You search the Scriptures because you think that in them you have eternal life; and it is they that bear witness about me, yet you refuse to come to me that you may have life. . . . For if you believed Moses, you would believe me; for he wrote of me. But if you do not believe his writings, how will you believe my words? (5v39–40, 46–47)

"*He* wrote of *me*." According to Jesus, Moses was writing about Him (this village carpenter from obscure Nazareth) centuries before—fourteen centuries or so before! Now, there's a claim to reckon with—this is either delusion or divine self-disclosure! Later in the story, on the day that Jesus defeats death and gets up out of the grave that couldn't hold Him, He goes on a seven-mile evening walk with two discouraged apprentices who have lost the plot. In Luke 24v25–27, Jesus says to them:

> "O foolish ones, and slow of heart to believe all that the prophets have spoken! Was it not necessary that the Christ should suffer these things and enter into his glory?" And beginning with Moses and all the Prophets, he interpreted to them in all the Scriptures the things concerning himself.

This Easter twilight encounter tells us it was of first importance for Jesus to help His apprentices see that the Scriptures cohere in a way that leads to Him. The phrase "Moses and all the prophets" was a common idiom for summing up the entirety of the *Tanakh*[13]—what is commonly called the Old Testament or Hebrew Scriptures. The point is, Jesus teaches us how to reread the Scriptures. He cracks the code on how all the seemingly disparate pieces come together.

He is what the prophecies and promises pointed to all along. All of Scripture's forward leanings land at Him like all a day's light is traced back to the sun. He is the substance to which the shadows pointed. All its promises find their amen, their "yes, it is true" in Him.[14] This means that meditating on Scripture is a crucial way of sitting at the feet of the Master to learn about Him, to steep in His wisdom and observe His ways. Scripture meditation is a fundamental way in which we abide with Jesus and learn to obey Him some two thousand years after He walked around Galilee.

TOOLS FOR MEDITATION

Apprentices of Jesus are to practice Scripture meditation day and night. But how? How do we go about hagah-ing this God-breathed, humanity-penned, story-shaped library that leads us to Jesus?

---

13 *TaNaKh* is a word used to refer to the Old Testament. It is an acronym for Torah (that's the *Ta*); Nevi'im (*Na*), which means "Prophets"; and Ketuvim (*Kh*), which means "Writings."

14 2 Corinthians 1v20.

Set Aside Time

Intimacy and intentionality are intricately linked. Prioritize by planning. Scripture meditation will not happen by drift, at least not at first. As apprentices of Jesus have done for centuries, we are wise to connect our rhythms of Scripture meditation with the rhythms of the day. As with eating, think morning, afternoon, and evening. Begin your morning with a planned meal of meditation on God's Word; start your day with divine caloric intake. Just as we plan for and await lunch each day, plan for hagah-ing Scripture in the afternoon, resetting your busied mind to the realities of God and His kingdom. In the evening, return again to what God has said. Like the story-disoriented and downhearted disciples on that Easter evening walk with Jesus, let Him show you who He is through His Word. Hear again the truest story of reality. This means being intentional about going analog before bedtime. Less Netflix and more Numbers or Nehemiah. Substitute a show with some psalms. The reality is, we make time for those things most important to us. Scripture meditation was of incalculable importance to Jesus. Does it shape your days like it did His?

Slow Down and Do It Again

In short, savor and repeat. In a harried culture constantly barking at us that there is not enough time to do all the things we want to do, we are bullied into rushing through the things that should be reflected on. Yet freedom comes only in un-rushed, deliberate movement. You cannot microwave seeds into a forest. You cannot speed up a pregnancy. You cannot expedite properly smoked brisket. We must habitually remind ourselves to slow down and savor. We are not in a race to consume Jesus data. He will not be constrained to ones and zeros and sound bites. We are to meet Him unhurriedly through attention to His Word. Wisdom is ever at odds with impatience. Intimacy is ever at odds with haste. We are to steep in the Scriptures. And then . . . we do it again. In repetition there is cultivation of an inner life. In repetition there is internalization, assimilation. This runs counter to our culture's novelty addiction, which is allergic to repetition and produces an exhausting superficiality, a frantic skimming across the surface of the waters of wisdom. Meditation is not waterskiing. It is the slow exploration of ocean depths—that's where wonders of exotic life and ancient treasure lie hidden.

The deep-down things of life take time to rise.

Speak It Aloud

Scripture should be on our lips. Rabbis have long taught that speaking Scripture aloud helps it to become clear in the mind of the student while planting it in the field of the heart. The spoken word is sacred, and the voice (*qol* in Hebrew[15]) is an embodied way of connecting with the God who spoke creation into being. Neuroscience teaches us that when both auditory and verbal channels work together to process some-

---

15 Ludwig Koehler, Walter Baumgartner, and Johann J. Stamm, *The Hebrew and Aramaic Lexicon of the Old Testament*, rev. ed., vol. 3 (Brill, 1999), 1083–86.

thing, more neural pathways are created for the information to be encoded. The act of speaking brings about active participation and enhanced attention that helps the information take root. Also, it turns out we are wired for poetry and song. Natural and crafted rhythms of speech help ingrain information. It is why we teach our children the alphabet with a song. It is why you still know the lyrics of some jingle that was played ad nauseam on the radio when you were young. The tongue and lips are the gymnasium of memorization.

Memorize It

Instill what is lovely and real into your unconscious mind. Embed Scripture into reflex and recall so it can be drawn from the well of your soul in a moment. In Psalm 119v11 we read, "I have stored up your word in my heart, that I might not sin against you." Don't outsource it to a device. Sure, with the devices in our pockets, we can look up a verse when we need to. We can navigate an app to parse the Greek or learn the original Hebrew with help from a chatbot. But these expediencies should never replace the storing up of as much Scripture as we can within ourselves. Memorization is not a data recall operation. It is the shaping of our interior landscape, and for the remembering of the things that make us whole.

Talk About It

We talk about those things that we love, and when we talk about them, it has a way of inflaming them, stoking the orange-white embers of our delight. It's as though the sentences we share are billows on the glowing coals of what has ignited our affections. Just talking about the new album by your favorite artist can have you hungering to listen to it again. A joy shared is a joy doubled, as the saying goes. Scripture shared is Scripture redoubled—turned over again in the heart and mind.

Lectio Divina

Lectio divina is Latin for "sacred reading." It is an unhurried and prayerful reading and rereading of a text that helps us meet with God to be transformed by His love. It is a way we let the Word of Christ dwell in us richly, bringing us joy and helping us love God and one another.[16] Here is a seven-part structure for how to practice it.

1. **Relax** (*silencio*) is the gentle turning from the clamor and motion of the day, a quieting of the noise within and without. It is the slowing of breath, the stilling of the body, the settling of the soul. It is becoming present to God and saying with one's whole being, "Lord, speak to me."
2. **Read** (*lectio*) is simply to read the passage slowly and out loud, letting the text speak. Don't rush to understand or explain.
3. **Reflect** (*meditatio*) is to read the text again and again, looking for some glimmering, for a word or passage the Spirit of God is drawing your attention to. When you

---

16 Colossians 3v14–16.

come across something that catches light, nestle in there. Linger with what you find alluring. Like a traveler who rounds a bend and stops to gaze at a sudden, breathtaking view, let yourself be drawn into the beauty before you.

4. **Respond** (*oratio*) is to let your heart speak through prayer. Don't go at this alone—God is with you. Acknowledge His presence with honest conversation. Ask Him to teach you, to guide you, to show you what He has for you in the gift of that text.

5. **Rest** (*contemplatio*) is to linger and savor. Don't move on quite yet. Dwell in the communion. Take the goodness you are hagah-ing into your heart. Sit with God and His life-giving Word. Let Him love you. Look upon Him as He looks upon you in love.[17]

6. **Return** (*reditio*) throughout the day. Return again and again to the word or phrase that found you. Let it become a refrain in your heart. Carry it like a song, like a seed. Let it shape your seeing, your speaking, your being. Practice the art of remembering.

7. **Repeat** (*repetitio*): Come back tomorrow. And the next day. Let this rhythm root itself in your life. Repetition is crucial to formation. Lectio is not a moment; it is a way. Habituate yourself to intimate communion with God through His Word.

Maybe at this point something you might call realism or skepticism has you thinking, *Great. That's a lovely Latin-savvy*

---

17 "I look at him and he looks at me" was once said by an anonymous peasant of Ars, as recounted by Saint John Vianney, quoted in *Catechism of the Catholic Church*, 2nd ed. (Libreria Editrice Vaticana, 1997), part 4, ch. 3, §2715.

process, but where do I get the time? Life is too busy. So I'll be blunt: There is no way around it—to be an apprentice of Jesus is to reorganize your life around being with and obeying Jesus. Which means we need to reorganize our life in order to be someone who meditates on God's Word.

Do you know what the greatest prioritizer of our time is? Love. Delight. We organize our time, we order our attentions, according to our loves and delights. One of the Hebrew words for delight is *chephets*—which means "to bend toward something." To lean toward it out of a desire to be close to it. To choose it over other things.

Here is the secret for a flourishing meditation life—it is right there in Psalm 1v1–2.

> Blessed is the man
>> who walks not in the counsel of the wicked,
> nor stands in the way of sinners,
>> nor sits in the seat of scoffers;
> but his *delight* is in the law of the LORD,
>> and on his law he meditates day and night.

Delight. Wonder. Allurement. Warmed affections and a God-enamored imagination. This is *chephets*—to bend toward that which gives joy or pleasure. When we delight in something, we find ways to rework our schedules around it. We give our attentions to what has our affections—and what we give our attentions to then shapes our affections. Through meditation, we are "transformed by the renewal of [our] mind."[18] What we meditate on leads to either flour-

---

18 Romans 12v2.

ishing or perishing, and we live in a world that is a battle-ground of competing narratives. Too often we meditate on the wrong story, listen to some voice other than the Word of truth, feed upon some modern echo of Satan's old "Did God really say . . . ?" Scripture meditation is an act of radical counter-formation against the onslaught of dehumanizing narratives. Apprentices of Jesus are those who practice listening to God's Word above all other voices.

God has spoken. The Word behind all words has called us to listen, to feast, to delight.

8

Unceasing Prayer

Talking to God First and
Most About Everything

Thee, God, I come from, to thee go,
All day long I like fountain flow
From thy hand out, swayed about
Mote-like in thy mighty glow.
                    —Gerard Manley Hopkins, "Thee, God,
                                I Come From, to Thee Go"

If you abide in me, and my words abide in you, ask
whatever you wish, and it will be done for you.
                    —Jesus of Nazareth, gospel of John

I live on the eastern edge of Livermore, where idyllic hills are
crowned with stark white windmills. Just minutes from my
front door is Brushy Peak Regional Preserve, a well-hiked
landmark. Brushy Peak itself is a rounded summit overlook-
ing the Livermore Valley in which I live. It is dressed in gold
grasses throughout summer and AstroTurf green during the
winter rains. Throughout both, evergreen trees cover the top
of the round, like a mop of hair on an enormous head. There
are old tales that these hills and their rocky outcroppings used
to be hideouts for outlaws on the run with Gold Rush loot.
That's rather fun to talk about with my son as we hike its

trails. It also makes it somewhat reasonable to look for treasure among the rocks, as we do. Who knows what could be buried there, or what coins could have been torn loose from some linen sack as a bandit was scrambling for a hiding place. It's possible, right?

As my son and I hike the terrain, we fellowship. As we walk, we talk. We commune. I delight in how he naturally asks questions or makes observations or requests something as we go along the trail.

"Dad, why are there fences here—I don't see any houses or yards?"

"Oh, those are fences for the cattle that graze up here . . . so they don't come down to our house and eat up our yard."

"Dad, did you go hiking here when you were little?"

"No, bud, I lived in Colorado. We didn't move here until I was thirty-one."

"Dad, look! Bones! Are they human?"

"Hmm . . . I hope not."

The questions are great. The wonderings are the stuff of life that lead to praise and exploring the contours of each other's soul. Sometimes my son will launch into outright praise: "I love how green the hills are!" or "Those big bubbly clouds are awesome—they are definitely my favorite!"

Other times it is his dependence that shows: "Dad, can I have some water? Can I have a snack? Can we go climb those rocks?"

And sometimes it is a plain old frustration or ache: "I want to go home." "It's way too hot." "I have a rock in my shoe."

All those questions, observations, praises, expressions of joy and pain—they happen along the way, don't they? They are not interruptions of the hike and fellowship; rather, they are how we experience the hike and the fellowship. They are the relational substance. They are the communion along the way. My son doesn't tug on my shirt and say, "Father, can we sit down and have a meeting?" He doesn't then sit down in some exaggerated posture that is a caricature of reverence, laying out his wants and praises in stilted language. If he did, I would think something needs to change in my parenting, or that heatstroke had finally set in.

When it comes to God, the conversation, our communion with Him, happens unceasingly along the path. Along the way, we can talk first and most to Him about everything.

- "Good morning, Father. It's Monday—and we have performance reviews at work. Give me a good attitude because I feel less than human right now. Help me to be patient and kind today. Help me to listen, to receive feedback well."
- "Father, why do I suffer these emotional sinkholes when I have so many good things in my life? Where do these micro-depressions come from?"
- "Father, help me forgive so-and-so. These painful memories are pummeling me today. Grant me some moments of peace before I attempt to lead this team meeting."
- "Father, the green-gold of this sunset—glory! And those

big bubbly clouds are amazing. Definitely my favorite. Thank You."

Do you see? Every event and circumstance is a potential portal to communion with God. It is as Brother Lawrence said in his classic work, *The Practice of the Presence of God*: "There is not in the world a kind of life more sweet and delightful, than that of a continual conversation with GOD: those only can comprehend it who practise and experience it."[1] There it is—continual conversation.

FIRST, MOST, AND EVERYTHING

Prayer is the language of dependence and the intended primary dialogue of our lives. It is the gift of an ever-present conversation coursing through our days like the exchange of oxygen and carbon dioxide through our lungs. This is why the apostle Paul says shocking things like:

> Rejoice always, pray without ceasing, give thanks in all circumstances; for this is the will of God in Christ Jesus for you.[2]

and

> Rejoice in the Lord always; again I will say, rejoice.[3]

---

1 Brother Lawrence, *The Practice of the Presence of God* (Epworth, 1939), 15.
2 1 Thessalonians 5v16–18.
3 Philippians 4v4.

Read poorly, these verses brutalize us, heaping guilt and shame rather than their intended comfort and peace. Take a moment to consider how damning these verses are if we have a joyless and perfunctory understanding of prayer. If we have fashioned God in the image of an intimidating and demanding CEO. Or a divine tech support operator. Or a grumpy, unpredictable, hard-to-please sky-parent. What if prayer is tragically reduced to being on your knees, folding your hands, or offering formulaic, ultra-religious-sounding language? If that is the substance of prayer, how is one to go about living life while praying unceasingly? It's rather hard to do your job with hands folded and eyes closed. One is bound to be dogged by failure in their prayer performance.

So what does it mean to pray unceasingly? Paul probably just means pray a lot, or at the very least, more than we do. But he doesn't really mean *unceasing*, right? *Unceasing* is a rather severe word. But this is no exaggeration—Paul means exactly what he says. The key is realizing that Paul knows prayer is not something that interrupts life; rather, it is the way we properly engage life, moment by moment. It is how we attend to everything. He sees prayer as something like the wings of a bird—not a burden that distracts from flight, but the very way the sparrows navigate the sky. He sees prayer as spiritual breathing.

Let's say I was to tell you that living people must breathe without ceasing. I don't think many would say, "But I can't do that! I can't spend all my time breathing! I have a life to live, things to do, groceries to buy, a paycheck to earn, a phone to doomscroll." Clearly, such a person is not understanding breathing as the nonnegotiable means of living. Breathing, the process of respiration, is governed by the autonomic nervous system—that is, it is happening all the time. It is wired into our bodies. Something similar is at play with prayer.

The practice of unceasing prayer is how we navigate all of life, by *talking with God first and most about everything.* The highest good of the human experience is communion, intimate fellowship with God.

CALL-AND-RESPONSE

"So What?"—you must admit—is a rather clever title for a song. It begs for engagement. So, *what?* What's the question? Is it even a question? What *what* is the song about? Is this the "so what" of cool detachment or a "so what" of eager inquiry? Is this a cynical world-weariness, an apathetic lethargy, an angsty Gen-X anthem, or the curiosity of a young child who wants to know what thrilling thing comes next?

"So What" is one of the most famous jazz songs from one of the most celebrated jazz albums of all time. It is the opening track on Miles Davis's album *Kind of Blue,* recorded in 1959. This legendary modal jazz treasure has something to teach us about the intersection of time and the eternal—prayer.

Paul, who was likely not all that well versed in jazz music, writes something that "So What" helps us to hear. When Paul writes "pray without ceasing" to the church of Thessaloniki, he is not making up things for them to do to busy up their lives. Rather, he is helping them to abide with Jesus and obey Him through the practice of *unceasing prayer*—a practice that marked the life of Jesus. Prayer was the way Jesus lived His days. He was always sneaking off to some isolated place to spend time with His heavenly Father. The reader of the Gospels will also find Jesus praying in front of His apprentices, praying over them, praying for them, or telling them that He has been praying for them. Jesus was a man of unceasing prayer. Prayer was His way of being in the world. It was not just a thing He did; it was how He did things.

But back to our song. Before you read the next part, go ahead and shut this book. Pull up your music platform of choice—or better yet, put the vinyl on the record player—close your eyes, and listen to the song. Give Miles nine minutes and twenty-two seconds of your day. I'll be here when you get back.

So, what did you hear? What you heard if you did indeed step away and listen was a brilliant song rooted in call-and-response.

> The call, the initiating voice, is the bass: *Ba doop ba doop ba do doo.*

> The response, the replying voice, comes as the piano and horns: *doo doot.*[4]

A back-and-forth is born and an iconic musical conversation ensues. Here, in the first few measures of this song, we experience a more biblical model of prayer than what commonly infects most of our imaginations and churches.

---

4 I promise you, the album version is much more moving and enjoyable than my sad scat transcription.

Life in God's world is always call-and-response. God is first. God is primary. God is.

He is, as it were, the bass of existence: *Ba doop ba doop ba do doo*. We, as His creatures—those who are conditional, who are here only because of God's preceding actions—well, our lives are like the piano and horns: *doo doot*.

He is first and primary. We are secondary. He precedes us, for His Word creates us. We are by nature those who live in response to our creator. We are His image bearers, and we are to live in trusting response to Him as a fish lives in and responds to the waters of the Pacific. This life of trusting response to God is what the Scriptures call *shema-ing*, as we noted earlier, and this shema is directly connected to *shalom*. Recall that shalom is not merely the absence of conflict and frustrations, but the harmonious integration of all things for mutual flourishing.

Call-and-response. This is extremely important because we often get prayer precisely backward. Like through some funhouse mirror, we see prayer upside down and misshapen, and such a distortion disorients our spiritual life. In short, too often we think prayer is our initiating a conversation with a silent and standoffish God, hoping He will respond. We act toward God and hope He does something. We think prayer is calling out for help and waiting for heaven to reply. An earthly call seeking a heavenly response. We assume prayer is like our picking up the phone, making the first move, ringing God for His attention that is elsewhere and on other things.

But prayer is precisely the opposite.

Prayer is ever and always a response from the creature to the Creator. Prayer is continuing a conversation that God has started. God has first engaged us.[5] God calls, and we respond. He started the conversation first by way of creation. He has put us in this place. Here we are, in God's wonder-filled world. Now, what will we do with it? Miraculously, we were born—conceived by the intimacy of other human beings; then, living inside the womb of another human being gifted to us, growing from the size of a poppy seed to the size of a small pumpkin at forty weeks. Now here we are. Inhabiting a world that has multicolored flying creatures playing about in the sky, a world with massive beasts that sing underwater as they swim along Pacific currents. Here we are in a world that has organic candy called raspberries and the magic of summer-evening thunderstorms and pulse lightning. I could go on and on, and I probably should for a bit. The point is, we live in a world born of God's Word and it demands a response. And not any old response, but a commensurate one of awe and gratitude and trust.

I should note that we are always responding to God. There is no way we cannot be responding, given we live in God's world that He is upholding moment by moment. The question is, *how* are we responding?

ABOUT VS. WITH

We can fool ourselves into thinking we pray far more than we do. Talking *about* God is not the same as talking *with* God. Thinking *about* God is not the same as talking *with* Him.

---

5 I can't help but to think of the line from Aslan in which he speaks of divine initiative: "You would not have called to me unless I had been calling to you." C. S. Lewis, *The Silver Chair* (1953; reprint HarperCollins, 1994), 23.

It is common to substitute talk about God for talking with God, or thoughts about God for fellowship with God. This "about mode" treats the other in a nonpersonal way, as though they are merely an object to muse upon, analyze, or gossip about, rather than a subject to interact with. The "think/speak about mode" is an *I-It* relationship, while the "with mode" is an *I-Thou* relationship.[6] When we fail to see the fundamental difference of these, or simply confuse them in our day-to-day life, we do relational damage.

Often, I get trapped in my own head, following labyrinthine synapses for far too long in the M. C. Escher–like corridors of my mind. I tend to make the mistake of thinking that just because I have thought of something I have communicated that something to someone who needs to know that very something. This leads to my wife saying things to the effect of "You know that I can't read your mind, right?" or "You may have thought it, but you never said it." Hmm . . . seems I needed to let her know that I was going to be out of town. Merely thinking about the trip was not all that helpful.

And I confess, as a pastor, muddling the "about mode" and the "with mode" is an ever-present danger. A devastating occupational hazard. I can spend hours reading, thinking, and writing about the God who took on blood and bone and a Middle Eastern complexion, and all the magisterial things He has done—breathing stars to light, bleeding forgiveness from the agony of the cross, rising from the dead, turning limestone hearts to tender flesh—only to realize hours later

---

6 The terms *I-Thou* and *I-It* come from the Austrian-born Jewish philosopher Martin Buber's well-known work *I and Thou*. In his work, Buber speaks of an I-Thou relationship as one in which we relate to each other as authentic beings, meeting each other as we are, not as depersonalized objects.

that I had not communed with the God who was there with me in my study. Imagine the absurdity of me being in the same room with my wife or kids for eight hours but never addressing them personally. I could think about them with the loveliest of thoughts, the most profound and honoring of contemplations, but without turning toward them, speaking to them, or acknowledging their presence, our relationship would wither in the lack of communion and intimacy.

Unceasing prayer is a life of *I-Thou-ness*. It is talking with God first and most about everything, not merely thinking about God when I happen to do so.

THE WAY WE PRAY

They had seen His way of constant conversation. They had watched as He talked to His Father first and most about everything. And so, His apprentices ask Him to teach them to pray. *How do we live this way of life?* Jesus then teaches them:

> When you pray, say:
>
> > Father, hallowed be your name.
> > Your kingdom come.
> > Give us each day our daily bread,
> > and forgive us our sins,
> > > for we ourselves forgive everyone
> > > > who is indebted to us.
> > And lead us not into temptation.[7]

---

7 Luke 11v2–4.

This is not a strict formula; it is a framework. A trellis for a grapevine. Jesus then begins to explain the heart of such a praying life by talking about a needy and audacious neighbor who knocks on your door at midnight, and a father who gives good gifts rather than a box of scorpions and serpents:

> What father among you, if his son asks for a fish, will instead of a fish give him a serpent; or if he asks for an egg, will give him a scorpion? If you then, who are evil, know how to give good gifts to your children, how much more will the heavenly Father give the Holy Spirit to those who ask him![8]

In other words, you must begin to imagine God as He is: God is your loving Father who, with a scandalous generosity, seeks your flourishing more so than you do. And if this is what God is like, then unceasing prayer is not a burden but a liberating joy.

Notice how the apprenticeship paradigm is at work regarding unceasing prayer: This intimate fellowship is possible because of *union*—union with Jesus makes prayer to the Father possible. For in union with Jesus, we now have the Spirit of Jesus, the Spirit of the Son, living within us.[9] And because of this, we are now empowered to *abide* with Him and *obey* Him. We come to prayer with a knowing that the Father has first said yes to us in Jesus, and He delights in hearing from us.

---

8 Luke 11v11–13.
9 Romans 8v15.

PRACTICING PRAYER

How then do we practice this kind of prayer? Here are a few ways that may help you get the practice of *unceasing prayer* written into your muscle memory.

First, unceasing prayer is a continual conversation made up of ACTS. This is a famous acronym—and I am so not an acronym guy. Nevertheless, this well-known acronym is true and helpful. ACTS stands for *adoration, confession, thanksgiving,* and *supplication.*

We should let our days be a continual dialogue filled with:

> **Adoration:** "God, You are good! I am amazed
>   by Your . . ."
> **Confession:** "Father, I messed up . . ."
> **Thanksgiving:** "Thank You for . . ."
> **Supplication:** "Grant me healing. Give me peace.
>   Help me . . ."

However, I think it would serve us better to alter this a bit. So how about this? Practice prayer with ACOAT:

> **Adoration:** "God, You are good! I am amazed
>   by Your . . ."
> **Confession:** "Father, I messed up . . ."
> **Observation:** "Look at that . . . I was thinking . . .
>   I feel . . ."
> **Asking:** "Grant me healing. Give me peace.
>   Help me . . ."
> **Thanksgiving:** "Thank You for . . ."

The changes here are the obvious reordering of words, changing the word *supplication* to *asking,* and the addition of *observation.* Most people have no clue what *supplication* means, so *asking* seems a more helpful word to me. And *observation*—do you know just how much bonding relational banter is done in the form of sharing observations and experiences? So much of the mingling of souls, of the deepening fellowship of friends, spouses, or family members is done through such sharing. To share an observation of an internal or external reality is a way we share ourselves and invite others into our hearts.

When my daughter says "Dad, look at that!" or "That makes me sad," she is not simply stating facts; she is inviting me into her soul. She is sharing herself with me. Sharing our observations, experiences, and reflections with God is not mindless chatter—it is treating God like a real being whom you desire to share yourself with.

It is also helpful for us to recognize that unceasing prayer is composed of both

1. **ongoing dialogue** occurring throughout the day, and
2. **planned times** specially set aside.

Every event and circumstance is a potential portal to commune with God. There is an unplanned, organic running conversation throughout the day. But that doesn't mean you don't set aside special times for prayer, or that there aren't certain frameworks or supports to enrich the intimacy and dependency that is prayer. Given the speed of life—and that massive corporations spend billions of dollars each year to attract and addict our attention to their products—we have to be vigilant to build special times of prayer into our schedule as counteractive measures. Just as we create a workout schedule and set aside time to go to the gym to stay fit, we should create a prayer schedule to train for godliness.[10]

My wife and I talk throughout the day. That doesn't mean we should never plan a date night to linger over a long dinner and share what is going on in our lives. Planning isn't being inauthentic; rather, it is being intentional about intimacy.

I talk with my kids throughout the day. Should I not also set aside times with each of them for daddy-son or daddy-daughter dates over breakfast or an In-N-Out burger?

I won't decide your schedule for you, as though there were one way to set aside sacred times of intimacy. But a good place to start would be to honor the rhythms of the day as anchor points for intimacy. Morning, midday, and evening are opportune times to schedule intimacy. They are three trellises in time upon which communion can grow, taking healthy shape and bearing good fruit.

Morning: To begin the first moments of the day by listening and speaking with God, acknowledging the grace of waking up, thanking Him for the night that has passed and the day that is ahead, and then sitting down to listen, to hear His Word—these are the movements that prepare us to live in the reality of a with-God life as we meet the deceptions and distortions of the day.

Midday: As the morning pivots to afternoon, as the sun reaches its height and we feel the need for food, we should let it remind us that we need to feast on God's Word and drink

---

10 1 Timothy 4v7–8.

in His presence even more so. To set aside some time—ten to fifteen minutes for a prayer walk, to rehearse some Scripture and then to respond—is a holy habit that helps us attune to God's presence with us. He has been there through the commute, the school drop-offs, the morning meetings, and He will be with us in the labors ahead and through the drowsy afternoon lull.

Evening: When the day of frustrations and joys is behind you, when the buzz and hum of all the tasks and texts are over, having an evening routine of being still and connecting the dots of the day to the God who has given it to you is vital. To help them not squander the gifts from God's hand and His presence, for centuries, Christians have practiced the prayer of *examen.*

Examen, another Latin term, is the practice of reviewing the day to retune ourselves to the sacred in ordinary life. Usually lasting fifteen to twenty minutes and done in the last moments of evening, the prayer prompts us to remember God's presence, express gratitude, reflect on the day, and prepare for the day to come. A simple five-part framework for examen is as follows:

1. **Attune:** Get situated and become aware of God's presence with you.
2. **Ask:** Ask for insight into how God was at work in your day.
3. **Review:** Examine what happened, what you felt/experienced.
4. **Respond:** Pray with ACOAT.
5. **Prepare:** Consider tomorrow and seek His counsel.

Most people want to check out after a long day of doing. And we are prone to do that amid the soul-sucking bluish glow of some screen. But rather than checking out, what if we were to check in with the God who is there, peer into the state of our soul, and enjoy the rest only intimacy with Him can provide?

REMEMBER: CALL-AND-RESPONSE, CALL-AND-RESPONSE

I find it strange how the brain can buzz and hum with so many thoughts, spilling over with opinions and flickering synapses, erupting with unexpected memories—yet when we turn our attention to prayer, it all seems to snap out of existence. Suddenly, nothing. Like the mind is a void, a mute and vast blankness. The desire to pray may be there, but the content is irritatingly elusive. Sometimes trying to pray feels like dropping a bucket into the darkness of an empty well.

But there is a full well to draw from. Like Jesus, His apprentices are to pray by drawing from the deep waters of God's Word. Jesus was raised on the Scriptures. He feasted on them, metabolized them into His bloodstream. God's Word was His native tongue. Recall, prayer is always a response, and so, as Eugene Peterson has said, "The reason why our prayers so often fall flat or come out stale is because they have been uprooted from the soil of the Word of God."[11] Given this, we best learn to pray and are primed to pray by praying Scrip-

---

11 Eugene H. Peterson, *Working the Angles: The Shape of Pastoral Integrity* (Eerdmans, 1987), 44.

ture. God has given His words and very self to us to help us give our words and very selves back to Him.

Here is a simple example of praying Scripture. As we saw earlier, 1 Thessalonians 5v16–18 tells us,

> Rejoice always, pray without ceasing, give thanks in all cir- cumstances; for this is the will of God in Christ Jesus for you.

These God-breathed words can then be breathed back to God:

> *Lord, help me to rejoice always. Even now in this pain, I re- joice. Turn my distractable heart and mind to You. Help me talk first and most to You about everything. Help me to be thankful in all circumstances, even in this wilderness of depres- sion. I know Your will for me, now that I am united to Jesus, is that I would always rejoice in You. I rejoice in You; help me to rejoice in You!*

PRAYING PROMISES

A specific way to pray God's Word is to pray God's promises. We see this all over Paul's letters. Almost all his prayers begin with praying what God has already promised. Apprentices of Jesus, those who practice Scripture meditation, will be those who have dwelt upon God's promises, and can therefore pray them in trust of God fulfilling them.

God promises in Psalm 32v8,

> I will instruct you and teach you in the way
>   you should go;
>   I will counsel you with my eye upon you.

So we can pray with confidence, "Lord, instruct me, teach me in the way I should go. Counsel me and keep Your loving gaze on me."

BREATH PRAYER

Another helpful tool is a short prayer synced up with the rhythm of our breathing. A breath prayer is often called a prayer of the heart because it is something that becomes re-flexive, something we begin instinctively to do over and over again.

> Heavenly Father, (Inhale)
> Your will be done. (Exhale)
>   —from Matthew 6v9–10

> The Lord is my shepherd; (Inhale)
> I lack nothing. (Exhale)
>   —from Psalm 23v1

> When I am afraid, (Inhale)
> I will put my trust in You. (Exhale)
>   —from Psalm 56v3

> Lord Jesus Christ, Son of God, (Inhale)
> Have mercy on me, a sinner. (Exhale)
>   —from Luke 18v13

Read through Scripture and begin creating a reservoir of these short breath prayers. Pray as often as you breathe. And when you breathe, pray.

ACCESS

Let's return to Brushy Peak for a moment. Not only are there rumors of hidden outlaws haunting its history, but there is a mysterious fence that prohibits hikers from exploring its wooded summit. There is a No Trespassing zone that sparks the imagination to wild wonderings: What treasures rest on the summit? To what secret and sacred things do we not have access? The first time I trekked up and encountered the unexpected fence, a warning sign hung on the barbed wires, and just beyond it lay a collapse of bleached cow bones, giving it all a rather numinous feel. Had I stumbled upon some small Mt. Sinai?

With some research, I discovered there is a sacred reason for the government fence. Beyond it lie gravesites and twenty-five-hundred-year-old artifacts of indigenous tribes. For the Bay Miwoks, the Valley Yokuts, and the Ohlone tribes, the verdant crest of Brushy Peak was a "thin place," sacred ground where the gods would rest, the people would meditate, medicinal herbs were gathered, and rituals were performed.[12] And so, this sacred site is protected from average hikers like me who might go tromping over hallowed ground.

Access to the sacred is forbidden for the everyday traveler.

---

12 A *thin place* is a location where it is believed that the boundary between the material and spiritual realms is thin or porous. The concept is often associated with Celtic spirituality.

And this reminds me of the miracle of prayer. Through Jesus, we have been granted access past every cosmic fence, every holy barrier in existence. Through Jesus, the fiery gate to Eden's garden[13] is again opened to any traveler on the mountain who trusts Him as "the way, and the truth, and the life."[14] Because Jesus is our High Priest who has torn the veil and "passed through the heavens," we have access to the sacred summit of reality, to the very throne room of God, and can "with confidence draw near to the throne of grace, that we may receive mercy and find grace to help in time of need."[15]

Prayer is the gift of miraculous, intimate access to the glad heart of God. Because of the reconciling work of Jesus, we can talk with God first and most about everything.

---

13 In Genesis 3v24 we read, "[God] drove out the man, and at the east of the garden of Eden he placed the cherubim and a flaming sword that turned every way to guard the way to the tree of life."

14 John 14v6.

15 Hebrews 4v14, 16.

9

Life Together

Living in a Confessing Community of Knowing and Being Known

> Love bade me welcome: yet my soul drew back,
>   Guilty of dust and sin.
> But quick-eyed Love, observing me grow slack
>   From my first entrance in,
> Drew nearer to me, sweetly questioning
>   If I lack'd anything.
>
> —George Herbert, "Love (III)"

> In coinherence, all things, all men, are bound together
> and co-exist, so that the life of each affects the others.
> Coinherence is not just union, it is the actual sharing
> of life.
>
> —Charles Williams, *The Descent of the Dove*

Something was shimmering into being. Taking on flesh. There was an electrifying rawness to it all. A wild generativity. A sense of adventuring, of wondering what would happen next. An easy gratefulness simply for its daily existence. No well-honed skill sets or professionalism to prop it up, to compensate for a lack of inner vitality. No fine-tuned blueprint for how it should all be done. Rather, it was carried along on guttural prayers of "Help!" and "What do we do now?" At times it felt to me like we were running along a canyon's edge, yet also like we were wandering through an open field. Like it could all fall apart any second, and yet, somehow, all would be well. And so we could be about the serious business of play.[1]

Those first few years of ministry in which we were clumsily cultivating a community of delight in God and each other were exhilarating, shot through with the endurance that gladness and purpose bring. Yet, without a doubt, the transition from plumbing into pastoral ministry was painful. For all the many times I split my skin open as a plumber, I have more scars from ministry. Even so, amid all the very real aches, there was the crackling energy of wonder wed with meaningful work, an ambient joy, and a deeply felt sense of being known. Imaginations were being baptized. Fragmented lives were coming together.

It is easy to let a nostalgic idealism distort the past and misremember what really happened—to gild the past with fool's gold, forgetting the rust and heartaches. Maybe I am guilty of a bit of unreal gilding here, but I think most of this is clear-eyed reflection years (and copious counseling sessions) later. In short, God granted us the grace of a deeply love-bonded community as this then very green pastor found himself in a pulpit and around tables of fellowship rather than in dark crawl spaces and out-of-order bathrooms.

In the fall of 2009, my wife and I moved from Colorado to the then-foreign world of East Bay, California. Hired to join the ministry team of Valley Community Church in

---

1 A nod here to a favorite line from C. S. Lewis: "Joy is the serious business of heaven." It is found in his book *Letters to Malcolm: Chiefly on Prayer* (Harvest, 1964), 92–93.

Pleasanton (a fitting name for the obvious pleasantness the city oozes), our commission was to plant and cultivate an intergenerational Jesus community. It was all a bit odd: a plumber-now-pastor in the technicolor land of all things digital and silicon. But, by God's mercy, a Jesus-apprenticing community was born through years of spiritual Braxton-Hicks and some brutal birth pains.[2] Week after week, I wondered if anyone in our ragtag crew would come back the next Sunday, or if the new relationships would hold together and become something more than veneers and acquaintances. Some did, many didn't. Yet with the two guiding principles of (1) a relentlessly open Bible and (2) radically open lives at the community's core, the upside-down kingdom was on the move. This quasi church plant was, in all its messy ways, a confessing community of knowing and being known.[3] We just didn't have those words for it back then.

First John 4v12 tells us, "If we love one another, God abides in us and his love is perfected in us." Love is at the beating heart of our transformation because love is at the heart of reality. Christlike formation is the outworking of love. And love is worked out, practiced, and exercised with others in community. We are changed, transformed, shaped in good and beautiful ways through love-bonded relationships.

Apprenticeship, by definition, can never be alone. It always takes place in community—a community of master and

2 Braxton-Hicks are irregular, often painless contractions that occur during pregnancy to prepare the uterus for labor.

3 This church community was called iNVERSION, a name that signified God was at work making us a right-side-up people in an upside-down world, and that we were to be a people in process (version 1.0, 2.0, etc.) as we were being transformed into the likeness of Jesus, degree by degree.

apprentice, as well as other apprentices. Apprenticeship always begins with union with another. And apprenticeship to Jesus is always in the context of a wider community because being united to Christ means we are united to the others who are united to Him. Our identity, our self-understanding and foundational orientation in this world, is inextricably rooted in our lattice of relationships. This is why loneliness, isolation, and disconnection tear apart the human being. It is why, for instance, one of the most diabolical tortures we can come up with is solitary confinement—the utter exile of a self from other selves.

The opposite of solitary confinement is the nursery. An infant is designed to be immersed in the waters of loving relationship, nourished in immanent presence, soaking in the joy and smiles of attentive parents, bathed in a bonding process that forms a sense of self and wires delight into their tiny little system before they ever learn to crawl. As authors Jim Wilder and Michel Hendricks write:

> Infant brains develop identity through joyful interactions usually with the mother and the father. The joyful faces of the parents are combined with the baby's growing sense of self to form a triad of joyful interaction. In this ideal environment, joy becomes the baby's strength, and lays a foundation for a lifelong joyful identity.[4]

These socio-neurological truths are theological truths. They are ancient truths given new language with words like *attach-*

---

4 Jim Wilder and Michel Hendricks, *The Other Half of Church: Christian Community, Brain Science, and Overcoming Spiritual Stagnation* (Brazos, 2021), 83.

ments, synapses, non-anxious, and *self-regulation.* They are words that call to my mind the Aaronic blessing:

> The LORD bless you
>   and keep you;
> the LORD make his face to shine upon you
>   and be gracious to you;
> the LORD lift up his countenance upon you
>   and give you peace.[5]

This God has turned His eternal delight toward us in the face of Jesus Christ, and He is loving us into a people who love. This means that to live a *with-God* life is to live a *with-others* life. And to live a with-God and with-others life is to learn to live in the ever-truer story of who we are as His people.[6] To be a people who practice life together: *living in a confessing community of knowing and being known.*

ETERNAL, MUTUAL DELIGHT

Why is the practice of *life together* essential? It's a bit like asking why water is necessary for a salmon or the sky necessary for a sparrow. It is because it is the natural habitat for that creature's life and flourishing. True community is not just good for us at some psychological level as an antidote to a

---

5 Numbers 6v24–26.

6 Dr. Curt Thompson, a clinical psychiatrist, talks about "believing the truer story" in a conversation with the Trinity Forum, www.youtube.com/watch ?v=8_ssOQq1hZQ.

lonely life or non-optimized existence. The truth is much bigger than that.

We are made in the image of a triune God.[7] A God who is three in one, one and three. One God, three persons: Father, Son, and Holy Spirit. Like some divine living musical chord, He is "three notes resounding from a single tone."[8] The co-inherent fellowship of who He is as an eternal and continual exchange of love. In other words, He always was; He always was love; He always was love loving. A God who is one and yet also a community is one of the great mind-widening and heart-filling truths He teaches us about Himself throughout the Scriptures. This means that a joyous community of mutual love and delight is at the very heart of existence.

In the garden it was "not good" for man to be alone. God creates Eve so there is a mutually loving fellowship among His image bearers that echoes His own communal nature. With these two human beings, alike but differentiated and mutually interdependent, God makes a small community of likeness and difference designed for flourishing. There is no shalom apart from love. Yet as we have seen, sin shatters that integrated garden community. Adam and Eve mistrust God, and a turning away from God ruptures their life together. The result: Human beings now hide from one another in the shame, and so begins the age-old pastime of blaming one another for how the world has gone wrong. Loving community is blasted apart. This is the photonegative of the apprentice-

---

7 Genesis 1v26–27.

8 A lovely line found in Malcolm Guite's poem called "Trinity Sunday: A Sonnet." Also, theologian, pianist, and composer Dr. Jeremy Begbie discusses this sonic-metaphor of a three-note chord in the book *Beholding the Glory: Incarnation Through the Arts,* where he and others brilliantly explore the interplay between theology and the arts.

ship paradigm: Rather than Union → Abiding & Obeying → Imaging, we are now caught in a doom loop of Alienation → Hiding & Autonomy → Distortion.

Yet, while in the disorienting wake of their sin, the One who is true community in Himself comes to meet them in their shame, calling out to Adam and Eve, "Where are you?" He knows full well where they are. His question is not data gathering, but a gracious invitation back into fellowship. The triune God comes to draw them out, to call them back into loving communion with the grace of His question. They will have no shalom in their state of disunion with God and each other. They sense their nakedness and feel shame—the soul's shiver of being "less." Their souls are out of socket. So are ours, if we are not united to Jesus and our alienation not overcome by love. We are designed to know and be known by God—to dwell with Him. We are designed to know and be known by others in loving communion. Our flourishing is found in His presence. And in His presence, we are to live out our calling of loving others.

To love others is to image Him. To image Him is to love others.

THE CONFESSION OF OUR HOPE

In the practice of life together, we are called by God to come out of our hiding, to leave the shadowlands of mask-wearing and enter the brighter world of abiding. Just as we see in the garden when God moves toward a broken humanity, it is through the grace of loving community and confession that we are healed of our traumas and relational ruptures. Sin shatters and then shame shields us from intimate communion. Out of wounding and being wounded, we self-protect to cope with the shame and pain. These protective measures are, ironically and tragically, self-destructive. It is as C. S. Lewis says in his book *The Four Loves:*

> To love at all is to be vulnerable. Love anything and your heart will certainly be wrung and possibly be broken. If you want to make sure of keeping it intact you must give it to no one, not even an animal. . . . To love is to be vulnerable.[9]

This is why the enemy works so hard in this world to buffer us from true community and plate our hearts with iron armor. He knows that in God's presence and through the presence of other Holy Spirit–filled believers we will have to confront our shadows, we will be held lovingly accountable, we will confess our need, we will become known, know others, and grow in knowing the effusive goodness of God. So Satan deploys relational smart bombs and barbed-wire barriers to true community. These attempts come in a thousand devious methods but can be categorized into the following three moves: *deception, distraction,* and *destruction.*

Deception

This is the diabolical narrative summed up in the line "I don't need the church." It is the lie that apprenticeship to Jesus, growth in Christlikeness, can be worked out with just you

---

9 C. S. Lewis, *The Four Loves* (Harcourt Brace Jovanovich, 1960), 169–70.

and God. That other people are only optional, only marginal in the story of you. It is a romanticized version of life (just you and God), rather than a *Fellowship of the Ring* mutually inter-dependent way of seeing the world.[10] It is found in deformed imaginations that believe online is good enough—*I can get all the teaching I need from the best teachers across the globe. It's efficient and comfortable.* But the church is not about data transmission or even knowledge. Never was. It is about trans-formation into Christlikeness, embodying love, learning to live well in God's world. Love is not made up of the efficient and comfortable. Rather, love is made of things like crosses and thorns, uncomfortable conversations and the pains of pa-tience. Just as one learns to swim in water, one learns to love in community. Someone can learn *about* swimming while sit-ting in an empty pool. But one cannot actually learn to swim until there is water involved.

Here is another deception in Satan's anti–life together ar-senal: shame. This weapon whispers hell-sourced things like, *You are too dirty! Better hide that real self of yours. You won't be loved if they know your whole story. Can you imagine what they would think if they found out what you have done—who you really are? No way. Get cleaned up. Figure some of this out on your own first, then get involved with a church community. Someday—yes, someday. First, get a bit better on your own.* These lies sabotage healing and keep the self locked away and moldering. And shame, like mold, grows in the dark hollows of the self-hiding soul. Its only power is in its secrecy. Satan

---

10 *The Fellowship of the Ring* is the first book in the *Lord of the Rings* trilogy written by J. R. R. Tolkien. The story follows the tale of a fellowship of hu-mans, dwarves, elves, and hobbits that need each other to overcome the evil that has ravaged the world of Middle-earth.

knows full well it is in community that we come into the light. Consider 1 John 1v5–10:

> This is the message we have heard from him and proclaim to you, that God is light, and in him is no darkness at all. If we say we have fellowship with him while we walk in darkness, we lie and do not practice the truth. But if we walk in the light, as he is in the light, we have fellowship with one another, and the blood of Jesus his Son cleanses us from all sin. If we say we have no sin, we deceive ourselves, and the truth is not in us. If we confess our sins, he is faithful and just to forgive us our sins and to cleanse us from all unrighteousness. If we say we have not sinned, we make him a liar, and his word is not in us.

Distraction

This attack on the goodness of life together is an aspect of what Jesus was teaching about when He spoke of seeds being choked out by weeds in the parable of the sower and soils.[11] Our vision is often crowded and crushed, our thoughts tangled with things like, *I don't have the time or the attention to give. I have all sorts of things I need to get done first.* The misshapen imagination says, *In this season we simply have too much going on to be engaged in life together. We want to set up our kids for success . . . so we are doing this hobby or these activities. My career is too demanding right now. Someday. Someday.*

---

11 This parable is found in Matthew 13v1–23; Mark 4v1–20; and Luke 8v4–15.

To these I would say, if you want to see your kids on the path of flourishing, don't model for them that a life with God and His body is optional. If career advancement has been ordered over and above abiding with the One who has given you the career in the first place, you have turned the gift into a killing thing. Even the best of employers and paychecks and Ivy League schools make cruel and terrible gods.

Destruction

This one detonates with phrases like "church hurt" and "another leadership failure." Satan is parasitic, so his go-to is twisting what is meant for good into a tool for grinding God's image bearers to dust. It is his perverted pleasure to take the things meant for the highest good and hammer them into weapons to bury God's people. Satan revels in beating plowshares into community-splitting swords. He takes glee in subverting the things meant for fellowship in order to sabotage the soul and the kingdom. Church hurt is a hellish sort of thing. It is like a doctor's scalpel used to murder rather than perform life-saving surgery.

Ever notice that the first murder was over worship? Satan weaponized the lofty gift of worship to spill a brother's blood. When Cain struck down Abel over their sacrifices, it was Satan striking at God by turning image bearers against each other. It is no wonder that so many churches have cracked apart over worship music. There is something to the snarky quote often attributed to Martin Luther: "When Satan fell, he landed in the choir loft." If Satan is a cosmic parasite, then he does his most destructive work with the most life-giving of things.

If deep love-bonded relationships are crucial in forming us on the journey toward Christlikeness, dysfunctional relationships also work to de-form us in *un-Christlikeness*. The inevitable friction in a community of in-process people provides an opportunity to embody forgiveness, long-suffering, and many of the other "love one anothers" found in Scripture. Or the friction can be an excuse, a way out, a self-justification to hit back: "No thanks—they are a bunch of money-grabbing, self-concerned hypocrites who never cared about me."

I don't write this glibly or with an air of dismissiveness or spiritual bypassing. And I don't write it to excuse or minimize any sin or church abuse whatsoever. I am a pastor, after all, and I understand this role brings certain power dynamics into the conversation. Yet I am a person before I am a pastor, which means I have tear-stained pages and confusing chapters of church hurt in my own story. But forsaking the church because of church hurt is like never eating food again because of food poisoning and a night of dry heaves. Terrible, yes. A sign you should never eat again? No.

And this is why the author of the book of Hebrews writes:

> Let us hold fast the confession of our hope without wavering, for he who promised is faithful. And let us consider how to stir up one another to love and good works, not neglecting to meet together, as is the habit of some, but encouraging one another, and *all the more* as you see the Day drawing near. (10v23–25)

In practicing life together, we *confess* that our hope is in Jesus, that He is our Lord and Savior.[12] We are to consider how to stir up (to provoke, to incite) each other to good works, to obedience to Jesus. We are to meet together to confess Jesus as King in our worship and to spur each other on in living as His apprentices. We are to encourage one another, pointing each other to the reality of a good God who is so for us that He took our cross and has given us life in the kingdom now and forever. And we are to do these things increasingly, "all the more" as history heads to its ultimate renewal and healing when Jesus returns. All the more. How's that going?

AN ANTI-COMMUNITY CULTURE

Not so well, actually. The number of Americans who said they have no close friends quadrupled between 1990 and 2020.[13] Fifty-four percent of Americans say no one knows them well.[14] The former surgeon general of the US has said that the number one health threat in America is loneliness, which the

---

12 The Greek word *homologeō* is used in this Hebrews passage to mean "to say the same thing" and is often translated as "confess" or "confession." The word is a combination of *homos* (which means "same") and *logos* (which means "say" or "speak"). *A Greek-English Lexicon of the New Testament and Other Early Christian Literature,* 3rd ed., rev. Walter Bauer, ed. Frederick William Danker (University of Chicago Press, 2000), 708, "homologeō."

13 Michele Majidi, "Number of Close Friends Had by Adults in the United States in 1990 and 2021," Statista, January 13, 2023, www.statista.com /statistics/1358672/number-of-close-friends-us-adults.

14 Rhitu Chatterjee, "Americans Are a Lonely Lot, and Young People Bear the Heaviest Burden," NPR, May 1, 2018, www.npr.org/sections/health-shots /2018/05/01/606588504/americans-are-a-lonely-lot-and-young-people-bear -the-heaviest-burden.

data tells us is more unhealthy than smoking fifteen cigarettes a day.[15] Cigarettes may give us lung cancer, but isolation is a cancer for our souls. All this in an age of so-called hyper-connection. And so the practice of life together is a diametric practice to the community-disintegrating ways of the culture in which we live.

Author and political theorist Yuval Levin describes the cultural moment like this:

> The ethic of our age has been aptly called expressive indi-viduualism. That term suggests not only a desire to pursue one's own path but also a yearning for fulfillment through the definition and articulation of one's own identity. . . . The capacity of individuals to define the terms of their own existence by defining their personal identities is increasingly equated with liberty and with the meaning of some of our basic rights, and it is given pride of place in our self-understanding.[16]

Sociologist Robert Bellah coined the phrase "expressive in-dividualism" in his influential book called *Habits of the Heart*, published in 1985. In short, expressive individualism is a way of seeing and being in the world that places the highest good on individual freedom, personal happiness, self-definition, and self-expression. We "author ourselves" and express that self to the world. The great irony is that such an individualist

---

15 Amanda Seitz, "Loneliness Poses Health Risks as Deadly as Smoking, U.S. Surgeon General Says," Associated Press, May 2, 2023, www.pbs.org/news hour/health/loneliness-poses-health-risks-as-deadly-as-smoking-u-s-surgeon -general-says.

16 Yuval Levin, *The Fractured Republic: Renewing America's Social Contract in the Age of Individualism* (Basic, 2016), 148.

approach to reality, such an enthronement of the self, breaks us apart at the deepest levels of our being, leaving us lonelier and more deluded. We have been sold a bill of goods.

When the self is radicalized into thinking it is the ultimate authority, the defining word on reality, it becomes the destroyer of both self and true community. Transcendent truth, beautiful unions higher than the self, and common moral goods are dissolved in the acids of the sovereign self. The celebrated ethic of our age is a destroyer.

One of the things Covid and the tumultuous years of 2020–21 highlighted is that we are irradicably relational beings—we need, we are wired for community. And when we don't have it, when social distancing is the way, our flourishing is undermined.

Recent research demonstrates the harmful nature of social separation. Studies reveal that individuals with less social connection have disrupted sleep patterns,[17] altered immune systems,[18] more inflammation,[19] and higher levels of stress hormones.[20] The opposite of shalom.

---

17 Ye Luo et al., "Loneliness, Health, and Mortality in Old Age: A National Longitudinal Study," *Social Science and Medicine* 74, no. 6 (March 2012): 907–14, www.sciencedirect.com/science/article/abs/pii/S0277953612000275.

18 Amy Ellis Nutt, "Loneliness Grows from Individual Ache to Public Health Hazard," *Washington Post,* January 31, 2016, www.washingtonpost.com /national/health-science/loneliness-grows-from-individual-ache-to-public -health-hazard/2016/01/31/cf246c56-ba20-11e5-99f3-184bc379b12d_story .html.

19 Yang Claire Yang et al., "Social Relationships and Physiological Determinants of Longevity Across the Human Life Span," *Proceedings of the National Academy of Sciences* 113, no. 3 (January 2016): 578–83, www.pnas.org/doi/abs /10.1073/pnas.1511085112.

20 Stephanie Cacioppo, John P. Capitanio, and John T. Cacioppo, "Toward a Neurology of Loneliness," *Psychological Bulletin* 140, no. 6 (2014): 1464–1504, dx.doi.org/10.1037/a0037618.

Another recent study found that isolation increases the risk of heart disease by 29 percent and stroke by 32 percent.[21] Another analysis that collected data from seventy studies and included more than three million people found that "socially isolated individuals had a 30 percent higher risk of dying in the next seven years, and that this effect was largest in middle age."[22]

Loneliness is also linked to accelerated cognitive decline in older adults,[23] and isolated individuals are twice as likely to die prematurely as those with more robust social interactions.[24]

In a *New York Times* article, Dhruv Khullar writes, "A great paradox of our hyper-connected digital age is that we seem to be drifting apart. Increasingly, however, research confirms our deepest intuition: Human connection lies at the heart of human well-being."[25]

In this culture of the self made ultimate, one of the most radical countercultural practices we can engage in is life to-

21 Nicole Valtorta et al., "Loneliness and Social Isolation as Risk Factors for Coronary Heart Disease and Stroke: Systematic Review and Meta-Analysis of Longitudinal Observational Studies," *Heart* 102, no. 13 (2015): 1009–16, www.heart.bmj.com/content/102/13/1009.

22 Julianne Holt-Lunstad et al., "Loneliness and Social Isolation as Risk Factors for Mortality: A Meta-Analytic Review," *Perspectives on Psychological Science* 10, no. 2 (March 2015): 227–37, doi.org/10.1177/1745691614568352.

23 David DiSalvo, "Loneliness Is a Mind Killer—Study Shows Link to Rapid Cognitive Decline in Older Adults," *Forbes,* July 25, 2015, www.forbes.com /sites/daviddisalvo/2015/07/24/loneliness-is-a-mind-killer-study-shows-link -with-rapid-cognitive-decline-in-older-adults/#9a305f4c37df.

24 Dhruv Khullar, "How Social Isolation Is Killing Us," *New York Times,* December 22, 2016, www.nytimes.com/2016/12/22/upshot/how-social-isolation -is-killing-us.html.

25 Khullar, "Social Isolation."

gether. So how do we enter into this practice of living in a confessing community of knowing and being known?

CONFESSING, KNOWING, AND BEING KNOWN

First, we must come to see that the practice of life together is not simply being around other people. It is not a practice of packing more social time into already overpacked and frenetic schedules. There are plenty of teams and clubs and societies and identity groups for that. It is being with other people, yes, but it is also being for others: being with and being for by being in Christ. It is not just a sociological thing; it is a spiritual reality founded on love and grace. It is what theologians called the communion of the saints—a sharing of and fellowship with the same Spirit.

Life together is the practice of living in a confessing community of knowing and being known. This means a community that

- confesses Jesus Christ as Lord
- confesses their sins to one another
- knows and is known by God
- knows and is known by others

To confess doesn't just mean telling someone the bad things you have done. It is more robust than that. To confess means to speak the truth, to say the same word (*con* = together, *fess/fateri* = to speak, to tell). To confess that Jesus is Lord is to say the same thing about Him that He, the Father, and the

Spirit all say about Him. It is to agree with reality. Apprentices of Jesus speak the truth about who Jesus is. And in light of the truth that He is Lord and that we are a people in need of salvation, we confess our sins, speaking the truth about what we have done and what we need.[26]

Not only do apprentices know Jesus as Savior, they know Him as *their* Savior. They know Him and He knows them. Apprentices of Jesus are learning more and more, degree by degree, who Jesus is, and they live in the widening joy of being known by Him. To be known by Him is to be loved by Him. He helps us unravel the mystery of who we truly are, shedding His light on the unconscious and unexplored oceans of our souls. No depth of who we are is hidden from Him, and yet He loves us to the bedrock of our being.

Every one of us wants to be known and loved; however, we often think being known and being loved are mutually exclusive. If we were fully known, we could not be truly loved—that is shame at work. And if we were truly loved, it would only be because we were not fully known, and so we must maintain the masks we wear. Again, that is shame running its mouth. This either/or works against the kind of community we are designed for. We are wired to dwell in a community of being known *and* being loved.

Let me share a rather personal case in point: Years back, I found myself in a brutal season of ministry. It was loaded with crushing cross-pressures, calculated betrayal, emotional confusion, adrenal fatigue, and unhealthy expectations (from others and from me) about what faithful pastoring looks like. Through a series of hits taken, paired with my failure of nerve

---

26 1 John 1v5–10.

to do some hard but necessary things, I began to curve inward. Piece by piece, I plated my heart with armor and detached the aching inner me from the outer pastoral persona. I felt that I not only had failed to serve the church well, but *I* was a failure, that who I was was a disappointment. So I buffered myself in the shame, short-circuiting the healing that authentic fellowship brings. I became a black box, sharing myself less and less. I stopped confessing sin and pain because I didn't want it weaponized against me. I believed the lie that being vulnerable had gotten me into that dark valley, and more vulnerability would only deepen the shadow. Loneliness fogged my soul. Imposter syndrome tied my tongue. I felt unknown and blurry. And my armored heart and unconfessed dis-ease sent ripples of anxiety and shadows into the community I loved. In short, I was no longer practicing living in a confessing community of knowing and being known.

This was one of the bleakest winters of my life. But by God's grace, I am miles from that dark valley now. Over time, others helped me see again the beauty of life together, their own vulnerability and patient love guiding lights along the way. The wounds from that season are now sacred, having been touched by Jesus through His body, the church. The white of those scars speak of cleansing, and of "the church of God, which he obtained with his own blood."[27]

Jesus loves us truly and knows us fully. The church is Jesus's body in the world. It is as Dietrich Bonhoeffer said: "The body of Christ takes up space on earth. That is a consequence of the Incarnation."[28] Thinking back to the apprenticeship

---

27 Acts 20v28.
28 Dietrich Bonhoeffer, *The Cost of Discipleship* (Touchstone, 1995), 248.

paradigm, *union* with Jesus means union with His body—the people of God. The twenty-sixth chapter of the Westminster Confession of Faith[29] states that all believers "united to Jesus Christ . . . have fellowship with Him" and are "united to one another in love." In Christ, we are united to one another in love. We are more than individuals within a local congregation with shared zip codes and service times; our membership transcends both space and time. Our membership is in Jesus Himself.[30]

Christ is in us, and we in Him. To love Him is to love others. To love others is to love Him. To walk with Him is to walk with others.

GET TO THE TABLE

Have you ever thought about how Jesus was constantly at some table eating with others? It has been said that "in Luke's Gospel, Jesus is either going to a meal, at a meal, or coming from a meal."[31] Jesus had a thing for gathering at the table with all kinds of people. And when He wasn't around a table eating and conversing, He was teaching others with parables chock-full of food and feasting. Tables and apprenticeship just go together.

If we are to practice life together, we need to get to the table. First, that means gathering for weekly community wor-

---

29 The Westminster Confession of Faith is a well-known Reformed confession of faith written in 1646 to provide guidance on issues of worship, doctrine, government, and church discipline.

30 Ephesians 2v18–22.

31 Robert J. Karris, *Eating Your Way Through Luke's Gospel* (Liturgical, 2006), 14.

ship. This is a sacred time in which God's children worship Him in Spirit and truth. Where we sing together in harmony and confess our out-of-tune living. It is where we hear God's Word spoken over us in the presence of His people. Where we come to the table of grace (the Eucharist, Communion). Where we can be counter-formed against the self-centered ways and distorted narratives of the world with the Word of God and liturgies of hope.

Getting to the table also refers to the shared life of the church throughout the week, day in and day out. Get to the dinner table with others. Get to the lunch table with others. Get to the breakfast table with others. Get to the coffee table with others. Be like a hobbit and get to the second-breakfast table, or the *elevenses* table.[32] Gather with a regular small group, a band of apprentices that meet weekly to feast on God's Word and good food. Get to the table of accountability with a small, trusted group with whom you can share the raw and unnerving parts of your soul. A safe table around which you can practice regular confession, walking in the light together.

Be prepared, though. Life at the table is messy. It is full of laughter, but also awkward silences, opposing desires, and loads of unwanted opinions. Almost every night, my family eats dinner together. We make it a priority to get to the table with one another. We prepare the food and then we try and wrangle four kids from the four corners of the house and yard to stop what they are doing, wash their hands, and get to the table—all in hopes of happy communion and some good food.

---

32 Elevenses are exactly what they sound like: snacks around 11 A.M.

I would like to tell you that once we get to the table it is all laughter and inspiring conversation. It is not. Not in the least. There is food dropped on the floor and parental frustrations about *why we can't just eat over our plates—that is why we have plates in the first place!* There are almost always water cups spilled. There is a high likelihood of complaining about the food and pining for some other delicacy like mac and cheese instead of enjoying the chicken kebabs that have been labored over. There are passive-aggressive comments and bickering about the most trivial things. There are preferences bumping into each other. There are interruptions, selfish bids for attention, flying opinions, and crying.

At this point you may be wondering whether I am talking about church life or the loud and messy Hardesty dining room table. They can be rather similar. They should be similar, as they are both honest family life.

Sometimes when you get to the table it is a chaos-fest and you hold on for dear life to love each other through the hurricane of emotions and complex family dynamics; other times it is Edenic, satisfying far more than your belly—and you find it is your heart that is full in this momentary foretaste of heaven.

10

Unhurried Presence

Being Present to God's Presence in the Moment He Has Given You

> And behold, I am with you always, to the end of the age.
> —Jesus of Nazareth, gospel of Matthew

> To have turned away from everything to one face is to find oneself face to face with everything.
> —Elizabeth Bowen, *The Heat of the Day*

Time and attention: They are the medium of devotion. In her luminous book of essays, Mary Oliver writes,

> Give them the fields and the woods and the possibility of the world salvaged from the lords of profit. Stand them in the stream, head them upstream, rejoice as they learn to love this green space they live in, its sticks and leaves and then the silent, beautiful blossoms. Attention is the beginning of devotion.[1]

Her lyrical words summon us to slow down, to enter the sacred gift of the present moment, to stop and savor for dear

---

1 Mary Oliver, *Upstream: Selected Essays* (Penguin, 2016), 8.

life, to fight with all our energies against the distracted life we know. Out of the heart's haste and cultural haze, we are called to attend. To *attend*—the act of being present and presenting oneself to someone or something.[2] We are all too familiar with being somewhere and some*when* other than where and when we are. Often, we are looking to the past or far ahead to some theoretical future, rather than awake to the charged *now*.

Time is a riddle to us. Like a house cat thrown in a river, we are ill at ease in time's flow. Our souls chronically suffer from a bad theology of time. From a misuse of the streaming moments that story our lives.

We often don't think of time theologically. However, a healthy relationship with time is vital for being an apprentice to Jesus. But what is time? This is a tricky question to answer given our familiarity with time and our often-strained relationship with its mysterious ways. Time, you might say, is the medium of rhythms and attention. So, to mishandle time, to mishandle your rhythms and your attention, is to mishandle your life because those very things indelibly shape who you are becoming. And time, it turns out, is chronically abused and neglected. Whole industries make their profits from encouraging the misuse of time and the mishandling of our attention, luring us to the shallows and the glittering places of hollow things. One of the great de-forming, soul-distorting, and destructive forces careening about in our culture is hurry.

---

2 *Attend* and *attention* are inherently relational words, speaking of the idea of directing oneself to, or "stretching" oneself toward, another. It comes from the Latin *attendere*, which is comprised of *ad*, meaning "to, toward," and *tendere*, meaning "stretch." *Merriam-Webster Dictionary*, "attend," accessed April 25, 2025, www.merriam-webster.com/dictionary/attend.

As author Pete Scazzero has said, "You can't live at warp speed without warping your soul."[3]

We live in a culture engineered to warp us with speed and the dazzling forces of distraction. Constant connectivity and pushy communications on our ever-present devices hijack our attention and bloat our desires to want everything and be everywhere. Social pressures and the hedonic treadmill of keeping up with the Joneses have us trying to run someone else's race rather than walking with God. Obsessive life hacking to maximize potential and optimize efficiency is not just in the water, it *is* the cultural water.[4]

Running from one meeting to the next with zero margin, having no white space on the scribbled-over pages of our lives, feeling the anxiety of having to innovate the next latest and greatest product to emerge from Silicon Valley, to land the biggest contract, or to be the alpha-parent on the block who produces the most accomplished Stanford-bound child. Side hustling. Neuro-tuning. Micro-learning. Gamifying. Doomscrolling. Habit-stacking. Biohacking. Flow-engineering. Life-optimizing. Hack-stacking-game-scrolling-opti-flow-

---

3 Pete Scazzero, *The Emotionally Healthy Leader: How Transforming Your Inner Life Will Deeply Transform Your Church, Team, and the World* (Zondervan, 2015), 129.

4 Jacques Ellul called this cult of efficiency *la technique*. Technique, for Ellul, is not just a tool or method; it is a posture of faith in efficiency as the ultimate virtue. This totalizing virtue says that whatever can be optimized should be. This belief has become the deep, organizing center of society, reshaping every field of human activity. In the preface of his book *The Technological Society*, Ellul says, "Technique is the totality of methods rationally arrived at and having absolute efficiency (for a given stage of development) in every field of human activity," trans. John Wilkinson (Vintage, 1994), xxv. In short, everything must be made faster, better, and more efficient—regardless of moral or spiritual cost.

multitasking-hustle-ification. Okay, now I'm just making things up to match the absurdities we have normalized. These things steal from us. Distraction is a great enemy of the soul.

So, too, is hurry. Dallas Willard has famously said, "Hurry is the great enemy of the spiritual life in our day. You must ruthlessly eliminate hurry from your life."[5] "Hurry," says John Mark Comer, is a form of "violence on the soul."[6] It is an enemy to our soul that is not only accepted, not simply validated, but is valorized, worn as a badge of honor, lauded as the virtue of the successful ones who live their lives up and to the right. But hurry is much more a villain than it is a virtue. It rushes in, steals, kills, and destroys.

Have you noticed how reflexively we chant words like "Busy! I am so busy!" If we stop the crazy-go-round for a moment to ask what is really being said when we invoke the merciless god of busyness, we will see there is a dis-ease in the self for us to reckon with. When you dig beneath the skin of the go-to word *busy*, there are words under the word: *I am working hard so I have worth. I am productive so I am significant. I am valuable—people are counting on me. I matter. Please, see me! Do you see me?* Too often the "I am busy" reply is an identity statement, a *who* (I am) statement rather than a *how* (there is a lot going on lately) update. This busy that we speak of is less "I am doing many things" and more "I am troubled—my heart is frenetic."

Why is hurry such a villain? Because hurry distorts our

5 Dallas Willard, quoted in John Ortberg, *Soul Keeping: Caring for the Most Important Part of You* (Zondervan, 2014), 20.

6 John Mark Comer, *The Ruthless Elimination of Hurry: How to Stay Emotionally Healthy and Spiritually Alive in the Chaos of the Modern World* (WaterBrook, 2019), 47. For an extremely helpful and in-depth exploration of hurry and its harm, slow down and read the entirety of John Mark's book.

humanity. It blurs our vision. It blunts our love. It is deformative.

It's no secret that when Formula 1 drivers are behind the wheel they aren't looking around and enjoying the beautiful scenery. Speed blurs the world and the people in it. One of the devious problems of hurry is that in the blur of the motion we often can't see that hurry itself is a problem. And when we are told it is problematic, our hectic hearts play defense and declare we don't have the time to address it. Then we go faster, doing more in an attempt to solve our discontent. But this is like drinking arsenic as an antidote to being bitten by a rattlesnake. Yet, denial, dangerous doings, and other defense tactics aside, we feel hurry's soul-sucking effects. As Shakespeare knew, "truth will out."[7] And the truth is, we are sick.

Psychology Today defines hurry sickness as

> a malaise in which a person feels chronically short on time, and so tends to perform every task faster and to get flustered when encountering any kind of delay.[8]

It is a behavior pattern characterized by persistent rushing and ambient anxiety. A feverish way of going about life. A jittery, twitchy posture of soul. It is not truly being *where* you are *when* you are or *with* whom you are. This means that hurry is an enemy of apprenticeship to Jesus because hurry is a dehumanizing force.

---

7 From Shakespeare's *The Merchant of Venice,* act 2, scene 2, line 78.

8 Rosemary Sword and Philip Zimbardo, "Hurry Sickness," *Psychology Today,* February 9, 2013, www.psychologytoday.com/us/blog/the-time-cure/201302/hurry-sickness.

Hurry, much like a drug, keeps us reaching for another fix, clamoring after a dopamine surge, living in a state of super-normal stimuli, keeping our cortisol (stress hormone) levels high, hurting our hearts, taxing our nervous systems, disrupting our sleep, rewiring our brains, and making scrambled eggs of our thought lives.[9] Many of us are addicts and we don't even know it. And because our bodies have become addicted to the rush of rushing, to truly un-hurry would mean we would experience detox-like effects. We are not meant for such an inexorably noisy and blurry existence. Hurry is a destroyer of shalom.

We are torn in many directions: a demanding job, a growing family, internal and external pressures to keep up with those happy, shiny, successful people on social media (never mind they are not real), the honey-dos at home, all the resident aspirations, dreams, and hobbies that we never seem to have enough time for. Filling every little gap of our day with another task, email, text, news headline, article, and 2x speed podcast—we are scrolling ourselves into oblivion.

Jesus has things to say about this. In Matthew 11v28–30, Jesus ministers to the hurried heart, to the dehumanized and the exhausted. He invites us into the good life of unhurried presence:

> Come to me, all who labor and are heavy laden, and I will
> give you rest. Take my yoke upon you, and learn from me,

---

9 Supernormal stimuli are exaggerated versions of natural stimuli, artificial or amped-up cues that elicit a heightened behavioral response compared to natural stimuli. For example, the artificial and exaggerated flavors of certain fast foods make natural foods seem bland, thereby creating a cycle of craving more and more artificially amped-up taste to satisfy one's cravings.

for I am gentle and lowly in heart, and you will find rest for your souls. For my yoke is easy, and my burden is light.

Jesus knows that we are often a chronically distracted, overloaded, anti-present people, and therefore not present to God's presence with us.[10] He knows we are unpracticed in the art of being fully present and fully alive.

A CITY ON THE EDGE OF RIOT

In a *Harvard Business Review* article, psychiatrist Edward Hallowell writes,

> Like the traffic jam, ADT [attention deficit trait] is an artifact of modern life. It is brought on by the demands on our time and attention that have exploded over the past two decades. As our minds fill with noise—feckless synaptic events signifying nothing—the brain gradually loses its capacity to attend fully and thoroughly to anything.
>
> The symptoms of ADT come upon a person gradually. The sufferer doesn't experience a single crisis but rather a series of minor emergencies while he or she tries harder and harder to keep up. Shouldering a responsibility to "suck it up" and not complain as the workload increases. . . . The ADT sufferer therefore feels a constant low level of panic and guilt. Facing a tidal wave of tasks, the executive be-

---

10 We are more than non-present. *Anti-present* means that which seeks to destroy the present by operating in a way that makes it harder and harder to ever be present. It is a way of habituating ourselves out of the ability to be present.

comes increasingly hurried, curt, peremptory, and unfocused, while pretending that everything is fine.[11]

None of that leads to better loving anyone! These symptoms are not evidence of the way of Jesus.

If you take a good look at the fruit of the Spirit spoken of in Galatians 5, the fruit that should be growing in our lives as we apprentice to Jesus, you will realize hurry hinders each one of them. It is in the blitz of haste that I say unkind things to my children as I rush them out the door. It is in the bustle of hurry that self-control falls apart to old me-first muscle memories. It is in the urgency of "all that must get done" that I stop seeing the person in front of me, begin treating them like an object to use or discard, and fail to love them in that moment.

There is a scene in the gospel of Luke in which Jesus addresses a case of hurry sickness.

Now as they went on their way, Jesus entered a village. And a woman named Martha welcomed him into her house. And she had a sister called Mary, who sat at the Lord's feet and listened to his teaching. But Martha was distracted with much serving. And she went up to him and said, "Lord, do you not care that my sister has left me to serve alone? Tell her then to help me." But the Lord answered her, "Martha, Martha, you are anxious and troubled about many things, but one thing is necessary. Mary has chosen the good portion, which will not be taken away from her." (10v38–42)

---

11 Edward Hallowell, "Overloaded Circuits: Why Smart People Underperform," *Harvard Business Review,* January 2005, https://hbr.org/2005/01/overloaded-circuits-why-smart-people-underperform.

Jesus has come to the home of Mary, Martha, and their brother, Lazarus (yes, *that* Lazarus). The text tells us that Martha is *distracted*. That is a pregnant word. She is "distracted with much serving," with much doing. The Greek word means to be pulled in many directions. Martha is bustling—she's Windexing, sweeping, prepping the fish, scooping the hummus, frying the falafels, cutting the cucumbers, plating the food—and at some point, her internal pressure redlines with frustration. When it does, she lets Jesus have a blast of her steam—eyebrows raised and hands on her hips, she tells the Lord of creation what *He* should be doing. His response is magnificent.

"Martha, Martha," He says. The double use of her name is verbalized compassion. It is a chorus of love. It is called an *epizeuxis,* which is a technical term for an expression of affection and emotional appeal (like when Jesus cries out "O Jerusalem, Jerusalem" and weeps over the city He loves). Jesus sees Martha. He hears her. He knows her. He cares for her. He tends to her hurried heart: *Dear Martha, I see you. I hear you. Beloved one, here is what is going on. It is not that your house is out of order. It is that your heart is out of order.*

Jesus tells her, "You are *anxious* and *troubled* about *many* things." The word *anxious, merimnas* in Greek, means worried or unduly concerned. It is the word Jesus uses in Matthew 6v25–34 when He says, "Do not be anxious about your life, what you will eat or what you will drink," and in Luke 12v25–26 when He says, "Which of you by being anxious can add a single hour to his span of life?" The other word He uses here, *troubled,* is electric and enlightening. The Greek word is *thorybazō,* which refers to a city close to a riot—frenzy on the edge of disaster.[12] It is often used to refer to the cause of an emotional disturbance or extreme agitation. Her heart is a city on the edge of a riot! This is hurry sickness circa A.D. 30.

Jesus is not simply addressing the stress of a demanding to-do list in the moment of hosting, but an internal state of hurry, a whirling chaos within the soul. Martha has just been diagnosed with a disordered heart, an anxious posture toward life and how its pieces hold together. The outward hurry and bustle are symptoms of what rattles deep within.

The word *hurry* comes from the Old English word *harry*—to make war, lay waste, ravage, and plunder; to overrun with an army.[13] To be hurried is to be besieged. Let that sink in. And Jesus lovingly diagnoses this unrest raging in Martha's heart. This brings us to an important point: Hurry is not being busy, as we might think. One can work very hard but not be hurried. One can have many things to do, yet not be hurried. This is because hurry is not found on a to-do list.

Hurry originates not from demanding external circumstances but from a disordered heart.

Martha doesn't simply need to *not host;* she needs to see reality anew. So Jesus invites her to unhurried presence, which her sister, Mary, is exemplifying:

Mary . . . sat at the Lord's feet and listened to his teaching. . . . "One thing is necessary. Mary has chosen the good portion, which will not be taken away from her."

---

12 Strong's Greek Lexicon, "merimnaō," Blue Letter Bible, www.blueletter bible.org/lexicon/g3309/kjv/tr/0-1; Strong's Greek Lexicon, "thorybazō," Blue Letter Bible, www.blueletterbible.org/lexicon/g5182/kjv/tr/0-1.

13 "Harry," Etymonline, accessed April 28, 2025, www.etymonline.com /word/harry.

Mary is stewarding her time and attentions with wisdom. Mary is practicing *unhurried presence:* She is being present to God's presence in the moment He has given her. The presence of God is the "good portion."

Unhurried presence is the practice of being present to God's presence in the moment He has given you.

It is to practice recognizing and resting in God's with-ness. In God "we live and move and have our being."[14] To be awake to this, to know the *with-ness* in which we live, is to enter into who we were created to be, to live from the deep-down goodness of things. It is to see by the light that is the light of all things. Time, like film, or a canvas, or a melody, is a medium in which finite human beings encounter the infinite and eternal God in a transformative way. These are deep waters, ethereal musings—so how do they take on flesh?

INTENTIONAL ATTENTION

First, we must direct our attention. There is a Hebrew word and concept called *kavanah*. Jewish rabbis have taught about *kavanah* for thousands of years, seeking to show that an intentional and focused approach should be brought to sacred observance. *Kavanah* means "intention." The root of the word means to direct or to aim. It is the idea of living with a holy intent. It is being attentive to God in everything you do. It is

14 Acts 17v28.

turning your attention to the awareness of God's presence with you. It is to have a God-saturated consciousness.

As apprentices of Jesus who are to be *being* "transformed by the renewal of [our] mind," we are to be attentive to what we are attentive to.[15] We are to think about what we think about. We are to treat God like He is God, and recognize that God is right here, in every conversation. He is with you on every frustrating traffic-packed commute. In every meeting and interaction at work. At the dinner table. While you scroll and post. While you take your morning run. While you read Scripture or the newspaper. While you have coffee with a friend. He is with you now as you read these words. He is.

Lord, here You are.

Unhurried presence is both as simple and as difficult as reminding yourself that He is present. He is here with you in this moment He has given you. This practice draws to our conscious awareness the good news that God is present. It is an integrative act of the imagination bringing together our affections, intellections, emotions, and will in a symphony of reality. As Herman Cohen says, "Kavanah is both emotional and intellectual devotion."[16]

PEELING POTATOES

Brother Lawrence, a seventeenth-century kitchen helper and sandal repairer at a Carmelite monastery in Paris, is well known for practicing unhurried presence. He called it prac-

---

15 Romans 12v2.

16 Jack Cohen, *Major Philosophers of Jewish Prayer in the Twentieth Century* (Fordham University Press, 2000), 14–15.

ticing the presence of God. Whatever he was doing—peeling potatoes, washing dishes, or sewing a new leather strap to Brother Claude's sandal—he sought to do so with the thought that God was with him, right there amid the potato peelings, crusty cast-iron skillets, and sandal leather.

The presence of the Holy One was to be found right there in the common business of life. Brother Lawrence wrote:

> Sometimes I considered myself before Him. . . . I beheld Him in my heart as my FATHER, as my GOD: I worshipped Him the oftenest that I could, keeping my mind in His holy Presence, and recalling it as often as I found it wandered from Him.[17]

In short, he directed his attention to the presence of God in the present moment.

He practiced thinking about what he was thinking about. Because of his union with God through the saving work of Christ and the indwelling Holy Spirit, Brother Lawrence could cultivate deepening intimacy with God through continuous humble attention rather than feverish doing.

So, simply put, practice directing your attention to the presence of God in the present moment. Remind yourself, mentally, verbally, that He is with you: *Lord, You are with me!* Habituate your mind, train it, that it might begin to reflexively say, *Oh, yes. Of course God is present here and now.* Enter into the way as is written in Psalm 16v8: "I have set the LORD always before me." David, who penned these words, lived with an obsessive God awareness, a God-saturated conscious-

---

17   Brother Lawrence, *The Practice of the Presence of God* (Epworth, 1939), 10.

ness, which is key to understanding how the not-so-perfect David was also a man after God's own heart.[18] Commenting on this verse, Dallas Willard has said that "the first and most basic thing we can and must do is to keep God before our minds."[19] Apprentices are to be attentive to the Master who is present.

ATTENDING TO RHYTHMS

A rhythm is a pattern of sounds and silences that creates a sense of movement and structure in time. Sounds and silences—an intentional interplay of activity and rest that brings order, meaning, and beauty.

By attending to rhythms, we can attend to God's presence. Rhythms speak to us of the order of God's design, and they function as regular reminders to help our amnesia-prone selves to think again of the God who is with us. To help in the practice of unhurried presence, think *daily*, think *weekly*, and think *yearly*. Let the daily, weekly, and annual rhythms that God has woven into creation function as signposts that lead us back to Him.

Daily (Night and Day)

In the opening chapters of Genesis, God creates the twenty-four-hour cycle we call "day." If you have read Genesis, do you

---

18 Acts 13v22.

19 Dallas Willard, *The Great Omission: Reclaiming Jesus's Essential Teachings on Discipleship* (HarperOne, 2006), 125.

recall the patterning for each day? It says, "There was (blank) and there was (blank)." How is the day ordered? The answer is not what we tend to think. The pattern is, "There was *evening* and there was *morning*." The Jewish reckoning of time is evening and *then* morning. A new day starts with evening and then progresses to daytime. But that seems backward. For us it is day that brings about night. In other words, we work and *then* we rest. But this inversed order we've adopted is no trivial thing—it betrays a whole misunderstanding of reality.

There is a meaningful order to how God has structured the rhythm of the day, and it is to shape how we reckon time. Evening and then day. Rest and then activity. Pastor and author Eugene Peterson talks about this:

> This Hebrew evening/morning sequence conditions us to the rhythms of grace. We go to sleep, and God begins his work. As we sleep he develops his covenant. We wake and are called out to participate in God's creative action. We respond in faith, in work. But always grace is previous and primary. We wake into a world we didn't make, into a salvation we didn't earn.
>
> Evening: God begins, without our help, his creative day. Morning: God calls us to enjoy and share and develop the work he initiated.[20]

Here again, we have call-and-response: God has first spoken, and our very nature as creatures is necessarily one of response. We need to re-imagine our lives in light of this sacramental rhythm of the day. The biblical rhythm of the day

---

20 Eugene Peterson, "The Pastor's Sabbath," *Leadership,* Spring 1985, 53.

teaches us, and reinforces with every twenty-four-hour cycle, that it is God who gives our souls rest; it is God who graces us with life and empowers us to live well in His world.

When we turn our days upside down, we break with the wisdom of the created order and restructure our world in a way that can only earn weariness, only bring a grinding down of the whole person. When we attempt to work *toward* deep rest, laboring to manufacture worth and earn an identity, we work against God's design and short-circuit the things that lead to flourishing. And as it is with the sacramental rhythm of the day, so it is with the practices of apprenticeship: Our efforts in training in Christlikeness are born of and fed by grace—they are not how we earn grace. The very phrase "how we earn grace" is a nonsensical thing that uses words and their meaning against themselves.

This gospel-rooted truth is found in the apprenticeship paradigm: *Union* with God precedes and empowers our *abiding* with and *obeying* Him. We don't work *toward* union. Union with God is a gift that empowers the process and the practices of transformation that lead to greater Christlikeness.

Weekly (Sabbath)

Now let's take this same biblical rhythm of a day and apply it to our week. In the Western world we talk about the *weekend,* which is a code word for not working. We hustle and sweat to earn our play and recreation. We see the week beginning with work and plodding along until we get to rest. Though common to think the week begins with Monday, it starts with Sunday, what the first Christians called the Lord's Day—the day of rest. Sunday is day one. Monday is day two, a day of labor that springs from and is empowered by our time of resting in who Jesus is and what He has done. In accordance with the world-renewing work of Jesus who rose from the dead on the eighth day[21] (Sunday, the first day of the week), His apprentices enter into the ultimate sabbath rest He has brought to the world through His work on our behalf.[22] And then, from the place of rest and intimacy with God, who upholds the world, we work, we sweat, we give our efforts to good and beautiful things.

I think here of an illuminating moment in *Moby-Dick*, which I have framed and hanging on my study wall. In a hunting scene full of sound and fury and frothing waves, the oarsmen madly paddle a skiff to close in on a whale. Sitting quietly in an uncanny calm at the front of the frenzied boat is Queequeg, the otherworldly harpooner from Polynesia. And here, Melville gifts the reader with this well-written bit of wisdom: "To insure the greatest efficiency in the dart, the harpooneers of this world must start to their feet from out of idleness, and not from out of toil."[23] Melville, it seems, knows something of the secret of sabbathing.

We are designed to inhabit a seven-day week with a twenty-four-hour period in which we cease from our labors. It is called Sabbath. Sabbath comes from the Hebrew word

---

21 Early Christian theologians dubbed Sunday the "eighth day," the day beyond the seven-day creation cycle, because Christ's resurrection on that first (and thus, eighth) day marked the dawn of new creation—a weekly foretaste of the eternal Sabbath. *The Epistle of Barnabas,* trans. J. B. Lightfoot, Barnabas 15:8; Saint Justin Martyr, *Dialogue with Trypho,* trans. Alexander Roberts and James Donaldson, chapter 138; Saint Augustine, *The City of God (Book XXII),* chapter 30.

22 This is what the author of Hebrews writes about in Hebrews 4v1–13.

23 Herman Melville, *Moby-Dick* (Modern Library, 1926), 289.

shabbat, which means "to stop or to cease." The wisdom of the Sabbath teaches us to stop our working and worrying because God is the one who holds it all together. It is a twenty-four-hour-long sermon that preaches rest and delight in a God who delights in us and works on our behalf. Sabbath shapes us to say, "You are God. I am not. This world will keep spinning even when I am not working." Returning to Genesis 1 and 2 for a moment, we see that God worked six days and rested on the seventh. Man and woman are created on the sixth day. The implication is that humanity's first full day of living in this world is one of rest and delight in God, and from that home base of abiding in rest and delight that forms identity and purpose, work then arises. Labor is born not out of anxiety and confusion but out of peace and purpose. But, like our disrupting of the divine rhythms of a day, we have turned the gift of a week backward and upside down. Unholy striving orders our days and misshapes our souls.

What is a week anyway? By the numbers, a week is a rhythm of seven days—or 168 hours, 10,080 minutes, or 604,800 seconds, to be exact. Why is this? Couldn't another rhythm of days, another set of hours and minutes govern our lives? Why is the seven-day week so pervasive throughout cultures and history? What if we could rewire it? What if we could restructure it to optimize our lives? People have tried, and it has been an epic failure every time. It did not go well for the French when the bloody revolution introduced a ten-day workweek in 1793 as part of a broader effort to de-Christianize time. And the Soviet Union's 1929 (five-day week) and 1931 (six-day week) attempts to rewire the week to support Communist ideology were disastrous at every level.

The seven-day week is not merely a tradition to be manipulated and optimized, but an irreducible divine principle for human flourishing. And now, a century after that last failed restructuring of the week, our age of dis-integration has us forgetting and repeating these mistakes. Our hyper-connection to technology and the diabolical pace and pressures of our culture has us laboring seven days a week to keep up, to not be left behind, to optimize our productivity, to maximize our output—and it is killing us.

Jesus and the Sabbath

Jesus tells us that "the Sabbath was made for man, not man for the Sabbath."[24] It is not a crushing command that requires something of us. It is not a weekly legalism. It is a liturgy of freedom. Recall, Jesus's yoke is easy, not crushing. Sabbath rest is one of the Ten Commandments given by God to His people that they might learn to live as those who are free from slavery. In Exodus 20v9–10 we see that the Sabbath is set apart or dedicated "to the Lord." In this Exodus account the Sabbath command is rooted in the creation order. Later, in Deuteronomy 5v12–15, the Sabbath command is linked to redemption and the exodus out of slavery. In other words, Sabbath is about the shalom we are created for and the shalom we are saved into as we are called out of death and exile. Leviticus 23v3 tells us the Sabbath is holy. A holy rhythm of time and attention that is meant for our good and the deep formation of Christlikeness in us.

---

24 Mark 2v27.

So, it is not just a day off. Sabbath isn't simply not working at your job. It is a radical turning of our attention to God, making space to delight in Him, and for play and enjoyment of the good things of His world that turn our hearts back to Him. It is a day of remembering who we are: a beloved child of our heavenly Father who gives good gifts. It is a day of worshipping through glad feasting and celebration.

Dedicate a twenty-four-hour period to stop and to delight. Unplug from the things that draw you into your daily work and duties. Turn your energies to the things that turn you to God and fill you with gladness. There is no one-size-fits-all way to sabbath. A good rule of thumb is that if you are primarily doing physical work all week, rest by doing something more physically relaxing and mentally oriented. Been running wire through conduit or laying sod all week? Slow your body and turn the pages of a book. If you are doing something mentally taxing all week and feel locked in your head, get more "into your body" on the Sabbath. If you have been crunching numbers in Excel or editing content all week, go on a run. Hike the ridge. Ride a bike. Get your hands in the soil, trim some roses, plant a tree.

Yearly (Seasons and Holidays)

As you go through the year, feast and fast in a dance with the seasons God has ordained. Let your year be oriented around Jesus, not just the sun. Organize your year around feasting and fasting with the church calendar.

Learn and lean into the beauty of a year beginning with

Advent, a time of preparation and anticipation of the Lord's first arrival and future return. Enter the joy of the days of Christmas, a prolonged celebration of the King's presence that brings light to the gloom of the world. Then be mindful of Epiphany, the weeks that take us from January 6 until Ash Wednesday. In these weeks we remember that the gospel is for all people, and that the revelation of Christ to all is signified in the visit of the Magi. Then comes Lent, a season remembering Jesus's forty days in the wilderness. It is a time to let go of comforts and distractions that crowd out intimacy with God. Holy Week turns our attention to the meaningful days leading to the crucifixion of Jesus. Palm Sunday, Maundy Thursday, Good Friday, and Holy Saturday are not merely for historic reflection, but for spiritual formation as we walk again with Jesus toward the cross that should have been ours.

Then comes Easter Sunday, the day of the King's resurrection when the new creation broke open into this broken world. The following seven weeks of Eastertide call us to live in response to the joyous hope that the grave could not hold Jesus. Next is Pentecost, the long-awaited day when the Holy Spirit was poured out upon men and women, marking the birth of the church and empowering the mission of God's people. This heavenly invasion ushers in what is called Ordinary Time—these are the days of faithful apprenticeship, of following the way of Jesus in the world, until the calendar circles back to Advent once more. Year by year, as we enter into the rhythms of the life of Christ, we are formed into greater Christlikeness as we feast and fast, sing and pray, getting the way of Jesus into our very bodies.

ANALOG OVER DIGITAL

In a world enchanted with glowing rectangles, be with the people you are with. Prioritize the person in front of you, honoring them as the miracle they are—an image-bearer of God worthy of your full attention. Don't shatter your fellowship by trying to also be with those who are not there, those who intrude into the moment with the buzzing, dinging, and ringing of your device. When we try to be everywhere at the same time, we are nowhere—we inhabit a shadowy half-existence. Use your tech to cultivate presence, not obliterate it. Let it be an instrument to focus attention, not a device of destroying attention.[25] Prioritize analog over digital, flesh and blood over flickering pixels.

The algorithms are constantly fighting for our attention. Don't be seduced into a soul-sucking semi-presence. Unglue your phone from your hand. Set it somewhere else. Turn off notifications. Uninstall social media and apps that are siphoning your attention and eroding your ability to be present to God and others. If you have an app that causes you to sin, pluck it out, cut it off. I'm pretty sure that is a direct command from Jesus.

Implement wise phone rules—or else the phone *rules*!

---

25 For a further exploration of this, I recommend reading Andy Crouch's insightful book, *The Life We're Looking For: Reclaiming Relationship in a Technological World* (Convergent, 2022).

BELOW THE HURRY

At the risk of sounding a little too conspiratorial, there is an ancient darkness that lies beneath the hurry of our hyper-distracted, overwhelmed digital age.

All this talk about hurry and attention and presence rests upon a key fact that we don't like to admit: We are finite. We are limited beings. We can't do everything. We can't spend all the time with all the people we would like. We can't be at every party, every event. We can't pick up or master all the hobbies that come and go. We can't exhaust the deepening seas of Netflix and Hulu. We can't reach the bottom of the infinite scroll.

We are finite creatures with glory-oriented limitations. And one of the great acts of trust in God is to recognize and honor our God-given limits. Some of us have a hellish time unhurrying because we have demanding diabolical wants. We want to devour the horizon. Yet, there is a wisdom of inhabiting our finitude. Joy is found in the humility of living as a dependent creature before an infinite God.

Theologian Karl Rahner once said, "In the torment of the insufficiency of everything attainable, we learn that ultimately in this world there is no finished symphony."[26] The world and God's cosmic purposes are far larger than us. The diverse beauties and inestimable goods of this world are wider than we can take into ourselves. The feast of existence is greater than our stomachs. We can't do it all or be it all.

---

26 Karl Rahner, *Servants of the Lord,* trans. R. Ockenden (Herder and Herder, 1970), 15.

We can't truly be anywhere other than where we are. We can't consume all that is or could be. And that's okay. Let us acknowledge our limits and trust God, turning our face to Him, and enjoying all that He in His wisdom has given us. Not coveting what He hasn't. Let us trust the particularity of His provision and be present to Him in the moment He has given us.

Remember, the great temptation Satan offered Eve was to bypass God on the way to Godlikeness. It was to sidestep her limits and the relationally paced process of spiritual formation God had ordained. It was to see something that wasn't hers and then to take it rather than receive it in trust and in time. It was to take into grasping human hands, to control and consume and gain the infinite knowledge of God that is only God's to give through His loving will. The great temptation was to be like God.[27] The temptation remains to seek Godlikeness without God-withness.

Beneath hurry is a rupture of distrust within our hearts. It is as Saint Augustine said centuries ago: "Thou hast made us for thyself, O Lord, and our heart is restless until it finds its rest in thee."[28] Until our trust is securely attached to Jesus, we will not know the deep rest that leads to flourishing. Our hearts will be like cities on the edge of a riot. We will suffer the blurry ravages of hurry sickness.

We are to be formed into the likeness of the King who brings the unhurried kingdom of heaven. The kingdom as

---

27 Genesis 3v4–5: "But the serpent said to the woman, 'You will not surely die. For God knows that when you eat of it your eyes will be opened, and you will be like God, knowing good and evil.'"

28 Saint Augustine, *Confessions*, 1.1.1.

lowly and potent as a mustard seed. Slow and secret as a pearl whose iridescence is shaped through the long-layering of nacre. Deliberate as a farmer watching the skies in a patient dance with soil and seed. Quiet as yeast eating through the sweetness of dough, giving rise to golden loaves.

11

Joyful Generosity

Gladly Giving to Others
What God Has Gladly Given to You

And joy, Grandfather would remind me, joy is the
infallible sign of the presence of God.
—Madeleine L'Engle, *A Ring of Endless Light*

The world is poor because her fortune is buried in the sky
and all her treasure maps are of the earth.
—Calvin Miller, *The Finale*

"There was a boy called Eustace Clarence Scrubb, and he almost deserved it."[1] This is quite possibly one of the snarkiest opening lines in literature. It's wonderful. Now, this Eustace is spoiled and intolerable. Or as Edmund, another character in the book, puts it, he is a "record stinker." To fill you in, Eustace gets magically drawn into a world called Narnia and caught up in a high-seas adventure aboard a ship called the *Dawn Treader* with some other children—Edmund and Lucy. Of course, I am speaking here of C. S. Lewis's beloved *Chronicles of Narnia* series. And this unpleasant Eustace, with a pathological self-obsession, helps us to see why Jesus talked so much about money.

---

1 C. S. Lewis, *Voyage of the Dawn Treader* (Macmillan, 1952), 1.

At one point in the story, while on Dragon Island, Eustace is out and about avoiding work, when he stumbles across a cave of dragon treasure. He is giddy with his find, quickly dreaming of how others would now serve him with his new-found precious power. After the adrenaline surge of his greedy frenzy, Eustace falls asleep on his glittering treasure with a golden bracelet he has put around his arm.

When he wakes up, he is disoriented and feeling rather off. Something is not right. It takes a few moments to shake off the confusion, but he soon realizes that he has been changed. Eustace is now a dragon. Scales, claws, and steam. And that golden bracelet he so gleefully wore is now cutting deep into the flesh of his swollen dragon arm. His selfish heart, his greedy "all-mine-ness," has changed him into a beast. What he thought would be his golden ticket to the good life has now curved inward on him. Rather than bearing freedom, his greed, symbolized by that golden bracelet, now shackles him with self-induced suffering.

I was seven years old when I first read about the dragoning of Eustace. This scene lodged itself deep in the caverns of my core memories with other stories of monsters, hidden treasure, and strange realms of adventure. "Sleeping on a dragon's hoard with greedy, dragonish thoughts in his heart, he had become a dragon himself."[2] That sentence has been with me all these years.

Okay, so maybe dragon tales and fantasy stories don't do much for you like they do for me. That's fine. However, what we need to see through the magic of Lewis's storytelling is the persistent principle of the deformative power of

---

2 Lewis, *Dawn Treader*, 75.

greed—and therefore the formative power of its opposite: *generosity.*

This is no unfortunate misstep for Eustace. His dragoning has been in process for years. This moment is simply the culmination of the desires and habits long cultivated in an unpleasant soul. A terrible tipping point. This dreadful transformation is the fruit of years of moment-by-moment, day-by-day formation. Eustace has long practiced selfishness, and now his body has taken on the beastly shape of his soul.

Might we be turning into dragons? It may sound silly, but that doesn't mean it is not true. We might not be sleeping on mounds of gold on enchanted isles, but this world is set on turning us into dragons. And in such a world, it is important that we be conscious of the formative power of both greed and generosity. If greed can turn us dragonish, generosity can make us more like God. For God is the most self-giving, generous being in existence. He is also the most joyful. On this, Dallas Willard remarked,

> We should, to begin with, think that God leads a very interesting life, and that he is full of joy. Undoubtedly he is the most joyous being in the universe. The abundance of his love and generosity is inseparable from his infinite joy. All of the good and beautiful things from which we occasionally drink tiny droplets of soul-exhilarating joy, God continuously experiences in all their breadth and depth and richness.[3]

---

3 Dallas Willard, *The Divine Conspiracy: Rediscovering Our Hidden Life in God* (HarperOne, 1998), 62.

God's joy and generosity are inseparable. They are like light and heat from the sun. The one is an expression of the other. Paul tells us in 2 Corinthians 9v7 that "God loves a cheerful giver," for God Himself is a cheerful giver and He wants us to become like Him. The word Paul uses that is translated as "cheerful" is the Greek word *hilaros,* which can also be rightly translated as "merry" or "glad-hearted." It is the way of God to give good things and to delight in the giving. There is no disgruntled blessing from Him, no sullen or annoyed act of redemption, no begrudging lavishing of His love. In His infinite goodness, in His abounding love, He gives without being decreased, without having less. His essence is eternal superabundance. He is a glad-hearted God on the move to make glad-hearted people.

Let's look at the larger text this cheerful bit sits in:

> Whoever sows sparingly will also reap sparingly, and whoever sows bountifully will also reap bountifully. Each one must give as he has decided in his heart, not reluctantly or under compulsion, for God loves a cheerful giver. And God is able to make all grace abound to you, so that having all sufficiency in all things at all times, you may abound in every good work. As it is written,
>
> "He has distributed freely, he has given to the poor;
> his righteousness endures forever."[4]

Paul's emphasis here is not to give more so you can get more for yourself; it is to give more so you can be more yourself—an

---

4 2 Corinthians 9v6–9.

image bearer of a self-giving God. Joyful generosity is not a theological get-rich-quick scheme. Rather, Paul is about the work of helping us see reality with grace-healed eyes.[5] Like Jesus, he wants us to intimately know the abundant love of God that shapes us into His likeness as we imitate His generous ways.

In the Sermon on the Mount, the great master class in teaching His apprentices how to live in God's kingdom, Jesus teaches us to look at the world through generous eyes—to see reality through an *abundance mindset* rather than a *scarcity mindset.* These terms were popularized in the late 1980s by Stephen Covey in his book *The 7 Habits of Highly Effective People.* Covey described an abundance mindset as one that believes there are enough resources and opportunities for everyone, which then fosters collaboration and growth rather than rivalry. He describes the scarcity mindset as one that believes resources are limited and that one person's gain will necessarily mean another person's loss, leading to defensiveness and competition. Covey's categories are helpful, but Jesus beat him to the punch by some two thousand years.

"Look," Jesus says, "see the abundant goodness of God your Father on technicolor display. Look at the playful birds of the air. They have plenty of food. Look at the lilies on these Galilean hills. Your Father has dressed them in royal fashion."[6] Jesus is working on His disciples' imaginations. This God who stocked the waters of Galilee with shining schools of tilapia, this God who has granted us the marvels of both light-

---

5 I was captivated by this phrase when I first encountered it in Philip Yancey's book *What's So Amazing About Grace?* Yancey attributes the idea to Irenaeus, the bishop of Lyons, France, who lived around A.D. 130–202.

6 Matthew 6v25–34, my paraphrase.

ning bugs and lightning strikes, this God who brings food out of the dirt and water out of the airy sky, is no stingy God. There is no shadow of scarcity in Him. No lack. No deficiency, no matter how much of Himself He profusely gives to others. He is, you might say, the opposite of miserliness. It is no wonder that Charles Dickens portrayed miserly Ebenezer as a man bound to death, haunted, being dehumanized in the collapsing world of his own tightfistedness. And it is no wonder that upon Scrooge's awakening, upon his Christmas conversion, he becomes a man of easy laughter and prodigal generosity. Generosity is incapable of scowling because it is too busy laughing at the amazing grace of it all.

"Don't be anxious," Jesus says. Don't panic and stress and grab frantically to get all that can be gotten, as if God's capacity to give is limited. Jesus teaches us to live in accordance with our spiritual DNA, to live like our heavenly Father who is a staggeringly generous host. Live generously; give joyfully. God is generous and His abundant grace is at work making a generous people. Joyful generosity is a crucial practice of an apprentice of Jesus.

> **Joyful generosity** is the practice of gladly giving to others what God has gladly given to you.

In order to help us practice joyful generosity, first we must see what is hard to see.

Greed is camouflaged. It hides itself from us. We are much more likely to identify other sins in our life than greed. Greed's self-protective tendency is to have us convinced we are more generous than we are.

Pastor Tim Keller once observed that no one had ever

come to him to confess their inordinate love of money, to admit their toxic lack of generosity. As a pastor, people come to you to talk about all sorts of things: petty complaints, crimes, anger, lust, gluttony, self-harm, addictions, you name it. But, like Keller, I cannot remember one time in my years as a pastor that anyone has ever sat in my study, nervously rubbed their hands together, and said, "I struggle with greed. It is difficult for me to be generous—there, I said it!" However, there was a gentleman who stopped by the church to let me know he would no longer be giving because "in this season we have to take care of ourselves." It was more of an anti-confession of sorts—I think. All this to say, greed is a shy and slippery devil. It doesn't like to be seen. It shrewdly hides in cost-of-living adjustments, unexamined standards of living, and self-justifying lopsided comparisons with other people.

Greediness is devious, flying under the radar, training our hearts to put our hopes in things that will undoubtedly fail us, things that were never designed to save us. And so Jesus, who knows the incalculable worth of a human being, has much to say about money. He wants us to see money as money, not as a master. He wants us to see it as a means by which we can become like our generous Master.

MOTHS, RUST, AND THE SECOND LAW OF THERMODYNAMICS

In Jesus's Sermon on the Mount, His shimmering manifesto of what it means to be an apprentice to Him, Jesus doesn't shy away from meddling when it comes to money.

Do not lay up for yourselves treasures on earth, where moth and rust destroy and where thieves break in and steal, but lay up for yourselves treasures in heaven, where neither moth nor rust destroys and where thieves do not break in and steal. For where your treasure is, there your heart will be also.[7]

At this point in the sermon, Jesus has been contrasting two different ways to live: the foolish life and the good life. And now, with money glinting in the spotlight, He again puts two paths forward: the way that leads to death and the way that leads to life.

> Option 1: You can lay up treasures on earth.
> Option 2: You can lay up treasures in heaven.

You can spend your energies investing for the short term, for the things you won't be concerned about while on your deathbed. You can worry over, labor for, and collect things that will wither and fade. Or you can invest your existence in what is eternal, in the kingdom of God that has invaded earth. A kingdom with no rust, no moths, no second law of thermodynamics to pull things apart over time.[8]

We know how to store up treasures on earth. We gather stuff and grow money in various funds and ventures. Many of us know how to calculate a winning ROI and cultivate fruitful portfolios. But how do you store up treasures in heaven? It sounds nice, but what in the world (literally) does this mean?

---

7 Matthew 6v19–21.

8 The Second Law of Thermodynamics speaks to the tendency of systems to move toward entropy, which is the measure of disorder in a system. In other words, things fall apart over time.

It means you live generously. It means you live like you truly believe that all you have has ultimately been given to you by God, and that God wants you to be like Him in blessing others.

This passage from the apostle Paul in his letter to Timothy helps us understand:

> As for the rich in this present age, charge them not to be haughty, nor to set their hopes on the uncertainty of riches, but on God, who richly provides us with everything to enjoy. They are to do good, to be rich in good works, to be generous and ready to share, thus storing up treasure for themselves as a good foundation for the future, so that they may take hold of that which is truly life. (1 Timothy 6v17–19)

There it is: "to do good, to be rich in good works." To store up treasure in heaven is not a wispy, pious platitude—it is the very earthy practice of using our God-given resources to seek the good of others. To generously give to those in need of the blessings that God has given to us. This is a whole-life way of being, not to be reduced to 10 percent of our finances given to a local church. To reduce the practice of joyful generosity only to what is commonly understood as tithing would be like reducing a marriage to the 10 percent of your verbal communication when you explicitly say "I love you," all the while giving 90 percent of yourself to anyone or anything else.

While we are discussing the practicality of it, I should mention a few ways we might channel generosity. Yes, giving to a local church community is up there on the list—that is low-hanging fruit. Do that.[9] There are myriad nonprofits that embody the love of Christ. We are also invited to share our resources with family, friends, and neighbors—with those who hold no nonprofit status and therefore offer us no tax break incentives. To help us along, it would serve us well to be praying and strategizing how best to set budgets to prioritize generosity rather than letting it be secondary or accidental.

We should also be thinking about what it is we might do without. There is a simplicity, a minimalism that is fitting for an apprentice of Jesus to live by, rather than the status quo of *excessiveness* fueled by rampant consumerism. What does a simplicity and minimalism that empowers generosity look like for you? It is a question we can't afford not to ask. Related to this is a simple practice of self-denial for the good of another. For example, practice not purchasing something you want, and then bless someone else with those funds in a wise way.

Ask generous questions. Get curious. Think and pray about how you might gladly give to others what God has gladly given to you. Ask these two questions of yourself and of God on a regular basis:

- Who can I bless with what God has blessed me?
- How can I give to others what God has given me?

---

9 And while you're at it, do some digging into the biblical roots of tithing. Take a look at the actual percentages that were given in the *Levitical, festival,* and *poor* tithes. When all are accounted for, the total giving starts to look more like 23.3 percent rather than a flat 10 percent. But don't just take my word for it; study it yourself. Here are some passages to explore: Leviticus 27v30–33; Numbers 18v21–24; Deuteronomy 12v17–19; 14v22–29; 26v12–15; Nehemiah 10v37–38; Malachi 3v8–10.

And here is an unexpected practice that just might be the most important way to cultivate generosity in our souls: Begin with gratitude. Gratitude and generosity live and breathe together. A glad heart, grateful for God's goodness, is the fountain from which rivers of generosity flow. If you want to cultivate joyful generosity, practice gratitude.

Begin every day with articulated gratitude. "Father, thank You for the gift of this day." Before your feet hit the floor, while you are still in bed, let the first words of the day simply be "Thank You." This humble but profound habituation of the soul toward gratitude will dig deeper and deeper wells of generosity in the human heart.

Speaking of gratitude and gladness, let's get to the very heart of the matter.

A CRUCIAL PRACTICE

It is true that Jesus spoke often about money. This makes some people squirm, others applaud, and many weaponize it. There is a reason Jesus returns to this topic often. He is after our transformation into people of greater love and joy, and what we do with money is deeply formative—and therefore has the potential to be dangerously de-formative. Money is not just something we do stuff with. Money has a way of doing stuff to us.

In Matthew 6v21 Jesus lays out an atomic axiom, a tightly packed and powerful principle on the formative power of money: "For where your treasure is, there your heart will be also."

This verse does double duty. It's like a precious coin: small in size, immense in value, and with two distinct sides. And for a long time, I saw only one. I thought Jesus was merely diagnosing the heart—giving us a way to take inventory of our affections, to audit what we love based on where our money flows. But He's doing much more. Jesus is not just revealing how our hearts are revealed; He's showing us a way through which they are shaped. This is not only a word of evaluation; it is a word of formation. He is giving us a crucial lesson in apprenticeship.

The first side of the coin reveals that our use of money exposes the heart. Think of those crime dramas in which it is inevitably suggested we "follow the money." The trail leads back to the person who committed the crime. The money gives them up, in time. Want to know what someone truly values? Want to know what, underneath all the things that are said, is of ultimate importance to them? Follow the money. Look at the budget. Examine the books. If you want to peer into their heart, look in their wallet. Want to know the true values of an organization or a church? Look at the budget and it will show you what lies beneath the sheen of the polished mission and vision statements.

Said another way, one's relationship with money is like an echocardiogram—a test that reveals the rhythms, the blockages, and the contours of the heart. But we can't stop here. The truth is more complex and more transformative than simply running diagnostics.

If the first side of the coin is like an echocardiogram that shows the state of our hearts, the second side of the coin is like exercise that actively trains and reshapes our desires, altering the architecture and long-term health of the heart. That's the second side of the coin I hadn't seen. Generosity is both diagnostic and developmental. It not only functions to reveal but also to reshape the inner person.

I imagine you have experienced this in some way or another. When we give to something, when we invest in some venture, we become more attached to it. If you invest in Apple stock, more than likely your attentions and emotions will be hitched to the ups and downs of the market. You will start tracking alongside quarterly earnings, product cycles, and market sentiment. You're no longer just a fan of good tech casually watching the latest keynote; you're tuned in because your heart follows your portfolio.

Feeling numb and wanting to grow in compassion for the poor? Wondering how to cultivate love toward those who are caught in a crisis? Start by giving. Invest in a nonprofit, support a missionary, or contribute to disaster relief. Open your chest and get involved with your treasure. Do you long to care more deeply about God's kingdom? Then give yourself to it—your resources, your time, your energy. As you engage, your awareness sharpens and your affections shift. Your heart begins to turn toward and be formed by what you give your treasure to.

Generosity is both a sign of a grace-changed life and a means by which God's grace continues to change us. The more we practice generosity, the more we practice being like Jesus. The more we live as stewards of the resources of a joyfully generous God, the more we are trained in the self-giving way of Jesus. *Abiding* with Him in His generous love and *obeying* His words of life lead to *imaging* Him. And this all comes from the fountain of *union* with Him. We love because

He first loved us.[10] We give with joyful generosity because He first joyfully gave to us.

Paul makes the formative power of practicing generosity clear when he says in 2 Corinthians 9v10–15,

> He who supplies seed to the sower and bread for food will supply and multiply your seed for sowing and increase the harvest of your righteousness. You will be enriched in every way to be generous in every way, which through us will produce thanksgiving to God. For the ministry of this service is not only supplying the needs of the saints but is also overflowing in many thanksgivings to God. By their approval of this service, they will glorify God because of your submission that comes from your confession of the gospel of Christ, and the generosity of your contribution for them and for all others, while they long for you and pray for you, because of the surpassing grace of God upon you. Thanks be to God for his inexpressible gift!

God's generosity toward us is aimed at making us generous like Him. He is after our Christlikeness. God gladly gives to us so that we might carry on His generosity and gladly give to others in trust of His goodness. And the ultimate example of the prodigious, glad generosity of God is found in Jesus. Paul links the call to be generous to what Jesus has already done. He highlights the organic bond of the act of obedience to our union with Christ. Appealing to the beauty of the ministry of Jesus, he says in 2 Corinthians 8v8–9,

---

10 1 John 4v19.

I say this not as a command, but to prove by the earnestness of others that your love also is genuine. For you know the grace of our Lord Jesus Christ, that though he was rich, yet for your sake he became poor, so that you by his poverty might become rich.

Yet the generosity of God as seen in the life of Jesus given to this world is not just an example to emulate. It is also a transformative reality that empowers. Paul calls giving generously an "act of grace" in 2 Corinthians 8v6–7.[11] That is, it is an act initiated by the grace of God and an act through which His grace works to shape us. As with all the other practices, we must keep in mind that our generosity is not a way in which we earn God's favor, but it is living empowered by His grace to press onward into its transformative power.

Why is the practice of joyful generosity so powerful in the formation of our souls? Because generosity works to turn the dis-integrative force of self-focus inside out. It is a denial of the self-destructive self. Generosity is an act of rebellion against the dehumanizing force of sin that denies the goodness of God and places self-concern over love of neighbor.

The love of God moves us out of the collapsing world of self-focus to the glowing horizon of loving others. It is the very nature of love to give—and to give back what it has been given. This is why the great symbol of love is the cross: the unbounded, ever-outward-radiating symbol of giving oneself for the good of others. Hebrews 12v2 speaks of this ultimate

---

11 2 Corinthians 8v6–7 is about the gathering of a collection for brothers and sisters in need. It says, "Accordingly, we urged Titus that as he had started, so he should complete among you this act of grace. But as you excel in everything—in faith, in speech, in knowledge, in all earnestness, and in our love for you—see that you excel in this act of grace also."

cross-shaped act of joyful generosity when it tells us that "Jesus . . . who for the joy that was set before him endured the cross."

Joyful generosity is a crucial practice of an apprentice of Jesus—a practical way of dying to self while letting others in on the joy at the heart of heaven: a glad God of eternal over-flow, of bright and boundless abundance, giving Himself away to usher others into the cosmic party.

12

Compassionate Gentleness

Stewarding Power with Sacrificial Love

Compassion is the other side of a living joy.
>   —Jürgen Moltmann, "Christianity:
>   A Religion of Joy"

He will tend his flock like a shepherd;
>   he will gather the lambs in his arms;
he will carry them in his bosom,
>   and gently lead those that are with young.
>   —the prophet Isaiah

His name was Oscar. I met him on a service call two decades ago. He was the landlord of a number of duplex housing units, and the unmistakably feared patriarch of a family business related to those ragged properties. Oscar was in his late seventies; he had a severe face deeply carved by decades of scowling. He had mean eyes, hair like dental floss, and a chewing-tobacco-stained chin. His sinewy arms jutted out from a yellowed T-shirt that hung loosely from him underneath his filthy overalls. He was the incarnate version of his lean, dilapidated properties. Or maybe they were the architectural image of him, like some real-life version of the bewitched soul-portrait in *The Picture of Dorian Gray*. Either way, the rentals mirrored Oscar: haggard, surly, surrendered to entropy.

He was locked and loaded as we pulled up in the plumbing truck. He blasted at us before we could open the doors. Though I had grown up knowing some rough-mouthed people, I had never met anyone whose speech was so effortlessly and impressively caustic, so acquainted with the motions of verbal abuse that it spilled out of him as easy as smoke rises from a factory. He was fuming, irritated that several faucets and toilets needed to be fixed. Angry that he had to spend money on us—"money-sucking, leeching plumbers," I believe were his words. Angry about having to finally address the complaints from his no-good renters. Angry about everything that was or wasn't or ever could be. He turned his salvo of words to one of his sunken-eyed grown sons standing discreetly nearby, sending him off on an errand with an insult and a grunt. And then, grumbling and muttering the whole way, Oscar walked us over to the first unit in need of repair. A quick look at the outside made me wince at what was waiting inside. Oscar ruled over a kingdom of de-creation.

The surprising thing was that Oscar had money. Loads of it. He had means. He was just a mean old soul who pinched pennies flatter than a railroad train.[1] He didn't use his financial means or the power he held for the good of anyone, it seemed. For years, he had practiced the terrible art of damming up love, holding back care, and unleashing contempt. King of his crumbling kingdom, he stood by us as we fixed a toilet that should have long been replaced. He loomed over

---

1 When I was a kid, we would put pennies on the Burlington Northern Railroad track that ran through town, waiting for the next train to smash the penny long, thin, and shiny.

us while we swapped out springs and washers in corroded faucets. He vented and steamed, careening from topic to topic—from politics to ungrateful wives to city ordinances to apocalyptic rants about "the kids these days" and hell-bound handbaskets.

I watched in a fearful silence as my father spoke to Oscar the whole time in easy banter, with gentle words, all while turning wrenches and stopping faucets from dripping. Calm and kind, my father took Oscar's vehemence like an ocean takes thrown rocks into its immensity. To my cringing wonder, he even disagreed with him, challenging him with lilting and resisting replies like, "Now, Oscar, that's not true. We both know that," and "Come now, that's just plain wrong." Somehow, he remained unbothered by Oscar's prickly words and dismissive grunts, meeting them with glimmers of laughter that lingered like soft light in the bleak washroom. Though it was my first time meeting Oscar, my father had been here before. He knew what he was walking into.

As we drove away, my father said, "Now, that Oscar—there is a soul who needs love. I can't imagine the pain in his story." As easily as he said it, he went quiet, into some long thoughtfulness, or prayer, or both. I sat in the strange, sacred stillness of the aftermath.

There, amid the entropy of those broken-down duplexes and broken-down souls, I witnessed abusive power colliding with a darkness-resisting gentleness. I witnessed in my father what C. S. Lewis once called "a bright patience."[2] Hallelujah.

When I read the words of Proverbs 15v1, "A soft answer turns away wrath, but a harsh word stirs up anger," I think of

---

2 C. S. Lewis, *The Great Divorce* (HarperCollins, 2001), 76.

Oscar and his life of whipping up anger and my father's responses to him that day. I don't know ultimately what happened to him, but I know that he didn't send us off with a cheerful raised hand of blessing, nor did he offer the faintest of smiles once the toilets were flowing and sinks fixed. But— and maybe it is only in my imagination after all these years of hoping in love—the grunt he sent us off with seemed to be charged with a bit less hate.

THE POWER OF GENTLENESS

In a fragmented world that has bought into the lie of a stingy God, it is common to see power and gentleness as separate things. Or worse, to see gentleness as the opposite of power. But in truth, gentleness is an expression of power.

Gentleness is the way of Jesus. He is the long-promised One who would not break a bruised reed or snuff out a weak wick.[3] There is a remarkable passage in the Gospels that teaches us this, one in which Jesus pulls back the curtain and reveals His innermost being with His words. No need for us to guess in the dark. He lets us peer into the holy of holies of His heart. He says in Matthew 11v28–30:

> Come to me, all who labor and are heavy laden, and I will
> give you rest. Take my yoke upon you, and learn from me,
> for I am gentle and lowly in heart, and you will find rest for
> your souls. For my yoke is easy, and my burden is light.

---

3 See Isaiah 42v3.

Through these words, we are granted incomprehensible access to see what lives at the very heart of reality: divine kindness. Jesus reveals to us that He is "gentle and lowly in heart." What is gentleness? And why is the practice of compassionate gentleness a fundamental practice in following the way of Jesus? To call out gentleness as an essential practice may seem odd, but that is exactly why we must bring it before our imaginations and get it into our muscle memory.

In an upside-down and dis-integrated world, gentleness is terribly misunderstood and contorted. Which is something the enemy of our souls is quite happy about and zealously invested in perpetuating. Gentleness is far more than a mild tone of voice or a quiet, mousy personality that we and the energies of hell have reduced it to.

I'd like to explore something strange. Something that might take us aback for a moment and make us rethink a few things. It is in the often overlooked passage that sits right before the well-loved text of gentle Jesus calling the weary soul to Himself. The magnetic words of Matthew 11v28–30 have a context, and we need to examine it to better understand this gentle lowliness of God. The opening words for Jesus's teaching are "At that time" (v25). At what time did Jesus say these comforting things about the way of His heart? Right on the heels of hard words. Words often skipped over.

Let's back up to verses 20–24 and see:

Then he began to denounce the cities where most of his mighty works had been done, because they did not repent. "Woe to you, Chorazin! Woe to you, Bethsaida! For if the mighty works done in you had been done in Tyre and Sidon, they would have repented long ago in sackcloth and ashes.

But I tell you, it will be more bearable on the day of judgment for Tyre and Sidon than for you. And you, Capernaum, will you be exalted to heaven? You will be brought down to Hades. For if the mighty works done in you had been done in Sodom, it would have remained until this day. But I tell you that it will be more tolerable on the day of judgment for the land of Sodom than for you."

Now, that's a hard passage most people don't want to stare into for too long. The Bible can be such a strange world to enter. At first blush, these words of Jesus don't seem all that "nice," do they? *Woe! Judgment! No more tolerating! Brought down to Hades!* Not the stuff printed on your standard coffee mug. And yet these words are set jarringly, disturbingly before our buoyant passage about rest and a Jesus meek and mild. It would be far more comfortable for us if these hard words were in some dark corner of some distant chapter so we didn't have to see them nestled right next to the words of a tender Jesus. This proximity forces us to reconcile these things.

What then does it mean to be gentle and lowly in heart? How can Jesus say what He said, dishing out woes and denouncing whole cities, and yet also be *gentle?* We must learn that gentleness doesn't mean never saying hard things. It doesn't mean sweeping evils and injustices under an existential rug. It doesn't mean never calling out error, forecasting rough consequences, or holding people accountable. It doesn't mean a perpetually soft tone of timid speech. So what does it mean? In this hard saying we see Jesus using His power for the good of others.

Jesus is not ranting and raving, casting fiery judgment from afar. He has come close in His love. Jesus has taken His ministry of teaching and healing to these cities. He has walked their neighborhood streets, experienced their sufferings. He has brought the kingdom of God to a dehumanizing and fragmented world, yet the people have rejected the very present goodness of God that leads to their wholeness. They are like those on a sinking ship who refuse the only life raft. And in His love, in the proper use of His power as the Messiah, Jesus shares His grief over their self-destructive ways, warning them of the consequences of refusing their only escape from the wreckage: God's Savior and the kingdom of shalom only He can bring. He uses the power of His words to help them see their desperate need.

"How sad! How terrible it is for you cities who have rejected your only hope!" He cries out. He has compassion on them, and His compassion is reaching out to them, warning them, calling them to turn around and walk toward life. Like a parent who aches with love for their child who is destroying themselves through an addiction, Jesus, in loving compassion, reaches out with the intense energies of love. His compassion for them is too powerful to not warn them with this intensity.

The Greek word translated as "gentle" is *praus,* which can also be translated as "humble" and "meek." It means that Jesus does not have a short fuse. He doesn't have an itchy trigger finger. It means He is deeply secure in who He is, knowing the mission He is on. He is in tune with the power He has, and how it is intrinsically bound with His compassion.

Compassion, too, is a commonly misunderstood word in a world of self-concern. The biblical way to understand compassion is to think of the guts—the deepness of one's visceral being that is moved with love, quaked with care. The Greek word is *splanchna*. It is a word of the vital organs, a marvelously intestinal and bodily word, and it is the source from which we get the word *spleen*. So, "love in the guts" is a good way to understand it. Compassion is to feel in your guts the ache of love for someone who is suffering. Jesus loved with His guts, with an ache shaking His core to see others flourish.

Being fully human and having experienced the cruel edges of a fragmented world, Jesus knows what it is like to suffer and be tempted. To register pain in the nerves and the soul. And so, He has the power to deal with us gently. Hebrews 4v15 says that He is "able to sympathize with our weaknesses" (*dunamenon sumpathēsai tais astheneiais*). I use the Greek here to highlight the relationship of power with gentleness, not to sound smart. That word *dunamenon*, which sounds something like the English word *dynamite*, has to do with power or ability. In Hebrews 5v2 we read that this heavenly High Priest "can deal gently with the ignorant and wayward" (*metriopathein dunamenos tois agnoousin kai planōmenois*).[4] Again, power and the gentleness of Jesus's gut-love are linked together.[5]

One of the most often used descriptors of Jesus in the Gospels is "compassionate." In Matthew 9v35–36 we read:

Jesus went throughout all the cities and villages, teaching in their synagogues and proclaiming the gospel of the kingdom and healing every disease and every affliction. When he

---

4 The Greek text of Hebrews 4v15 and 5v2 are cited from the *Nestle-Aland Novum Testamentum Graece,* 28th ed. (Deutsche Bibelgesellschaft, 2012).

5 For a thorough and helpful exploration of Christ's sympathizing and compassion, read Dane Ortlund's masterful book *Gentle and Lowly: The Heart of Christ for Sinners and Sufferers* (Crossway, 2020).

saw the crowds, he had compassion for them, because they were harassed and helpless, like sheep without a shepherd.

It is His way of being to *see* the burdened and the broken, the suffering and struggling, and to invite them into His heart that He may heal them. He feels with and for us. His love is locked onto the needy. It is His joy to bind up the broken-hearted and refresh the weary soul. It is as Saint Augustine wrote, "What is compassion but a kind of fellow-feeling for another's misery, which prompts us to help him if we can?"[6]

Jesus, if He had been there in all His blue-collar glory fixing Oscar's toilets and sinks, would have had gut-love for old Oscar—a gentleness to meet his toxicity and traumatized soul. "Christ is love covered over in flesh."[7]

YOKES

Let's go back to peering into Jesus's heart through Matthew 11v28–29. The passage begins with an invitation: "Come to me, all who labor and are heavy laden, and I will give you rest."

We have a Master, a Lord, who is welcoming. That is a wonderful thing, isn't it—to be invited in? To be seen and wanted. To not be left on the outside of love. Love invites others into its life. And who is invited? The soul-weary and anxious. The addicted. The stumble-tripping. The shame laden.

---

6 Saint Augustine, *The City of God,* book IX (Random House, 1999), 285.
7 Thomas Goodwin, *The Heart of Christ* (Banner of Truth, 2011), 61.

The regretful and haunted. Those carrying the backbreaking weight of being not all right. This is a call to all of us. To anyone bearing the one million tons of indwelling sin.

And what does this Jesus give? A cracked-apart heart put back into socket after a lifelong dislocation. A new life on the good road. And yet, this is not an effortless road that lies ahead. This promised rest and peace from Jesus come in the form of a yoke—a wooden collar, a carved harness put on oxen to attach a plow or a cart. It is an implement of work, of sweat and effort. The gentle compassion of Jesus comes in the strange form of an instrument of labor. Why?

A yoke is an image of union. If you are linked with the One who can do what you cannot, then His work is now marvelously yours through union. What's His is yours, and what's yours is His. A shattered humanity could not save itself. But Jesus could. As we are united to Him, His righteousness is now our righteousness, His divine life and work are now shared with us. The miracle of this with-Jesus life leads to learning a long obedience in the same direction He is going.[8] The practices of grace are how we learn to live with the easy yoke of a gentle Jesus. And that word *easy* doesn't simply mean "without difficulty," because the good road is often very difficult. Rather, it means kind and good.

Jesus is a brilliant teacher and His teaching is often multivalent.[9] In this passage, He is not just talking about fields and oxen; He is talking about masters and apprentices. *Yoke*

---

8 This phrase, strangely enough, is originally from the atheistic philosopher Friedrich Nietzsche, and was later used by the writer and pastor Eugene Peterson to describe a life of apprenticeship to Jesus.

9 *Multivalent* means having multiple facets, forms, or levels of significance.

was also a term used for a rabbi's teaching. Students would "take on the yoke" of a teacher, meaning they would link their lives with the teacher, walk in pace with them and take their teachings upon themselves. Jesus is telling us that His love for us has led to a healing union with Him, and in this new fellowship with Him, we are to learn to live in step with Him. Jesus says, "Take up my teachings, follow me, and you will have rest." He has used His great power and His great love to meet us in our need, to identify with us in our lowly condition. And He has invited us to learn His ways, for He knows the vicious alternative. He knows that people are harassed by cruel masters, by destructive religious impulses, tyrannical ideologies, oppressive cultural expectations, systems that abuse power, and dark powers that berate, burden, and afflict people. He knows that the yokes these things bring will destroy the people He loves. He knows that those ill-carved yokes will chafe and crush the necks of His image bearers with guilt, condemnation, and shame. He knows that they will bully, oppress, and dehumanize. And He knows that His yoke alone answers the prayer of Psalm 86v11–13:

> Teach me your way, O Lord,
>> that I may walk in your truth;
>> unite my heart to fear your name.
> I give thanks to you, O Lord my God,
>> with my whole heart,
>> and I will glorify your name forever.
> For great is your steadfast love toward me;
>> you have delivered my soul from the depths
>> of Sheol.

HABITUAL GENTLENESS

We have seen that gentleness is not simply a temperament, not a personality type that is only for a select few who won the genetic lottery. Any personality type, by God's grace, can and ought to practice gentleness. No strengths assessment or trending leadership test can be an excuse to bow out of the call to Jesus-like gentleness. Enneagram type 8? ESTJ Myers-Briggs? High D on the DiSC profile? Doesn't matter. Apprentices of Jesus are to practice compassionate gentleness.

This compassionate gentleness is not a smiling passivity. It is not simply being congenial or mellow. It is not fawning or avoiding crucial conversations. In no way is it being a pushover. Jesus never was—He had an adamantine spine. It is not talking in a soft voice or using only positive reinforcement. It may and should include some of these things from time to time, but in and of themselves they are not the biblical gentleness of Jesus. Gentleness is the submission of one's power unto and for the good of others.

The practice of compassionate gentleness is stewarding power with sacrificial love.

It is to use the power God has granted us for the good of others at cost to the self. We all have some power, you know. So the question is: How are you using the power God has given you? More often than we like to admit, we have abused our power. We have used the power we have been given selfishly at cost to others rather than compassionately in service of others.

Parents, you have God-granted power over your children. You are bigger and stronger than your kids—at least for a decade or two. You can intimidate with physical size and force and volume. You hold monetary power as well. You hold the power of affection, which can be easily and cruelly weaponized. You hold the mysterious but very real power of blessing or cursing—words of approval or rejection that work to liberate or shackle souls for a lifetime. How many of us are still desperately searching in every corner of our career and pursuits to hear words of a mother's or a father's blessing?

Children, you have power. You have the power to express love and affection, to honor and respect, or to withhold these things in cruelty or a form of manipulation. Have you ever snubbed your mom or dad, given a cold shoulder, or bent your words to use guilt or flattery to get what you want?

Employers, power has been granted to you. Have you used your position to bully and manipulate rather than taking the time to care for your employees, getting to know them as the people they are? To see them in all their hurts and their hopes? Do you push, prod, and coerce rather than serve, resource, and lead?

Leaders in all spheres, you've been entrusted with some form of power. Have you lorded it over others, wielding a title, credential, or string of Ivy League initials to diminish, dismiss, or coerce those in your care? Have you used Scripture like a mugger's knife rather than a doctor's scalpel? Is shame a tool in your arsenal to get people to do what you want?

For all of us—how have we used the power of our voice, our relational influence, our technology, our tools, our reasoning abilities? Have we used these forms of power compassionately, to love others? Or have we used them to punch back and score points while running along the tracks culture has laid before us? Have we ever abused the power we have to publish something on social media—marshalling our energies to pummel an opponent? Eviscerating others with our wit? Here now is a needed practice of compassionate gentleness: not always needing to have the last word.[10]

To be clear, I am not saying we shed conviction—that we muzzle passion, dilute truth, and never cry foul or call out error. Remember the woe proclaiming and the table flipping of gentle and lowly Jesus? True gentleness is bold and courageous and costly, but it uses its power to call others into flourishing, not cancel them by way of the feel-good anger and hate in our hearts. Tenderness is not the same thing as timidity—a lesson I wish I had learned long ago.[11]

So, here is my encouragement to you. Don't leave the things of power hidden in the shadow. Do a power audit. Ask:

- *What power do I have in the various spheres of my life?*
- *How am I stewarding the power God has given me?*
- *Where is my power use cruciform? Where is it self-serving?*

The best way to imagine the practice of compassionate gentleness is to look at its ultimate expression, to turn the eyes of our heart to the cross of Jesus.

On Calvary, Jesus faced nerve-numbing abuse. Though utterly innocent, He was brutalized and body-shocked. Mocked,

---

10 Dallas Willard spoke of this practice at the Knowing Christ Conference in Santa Barbara, California, in February 2013. This last conference of Willard's has been transcribed into a book called *Living in Christ's Presence* by John Ortberg.

11 2 Timothy 1v7 is quite clear that we are not given a spirit of "fear [timidity] but of power and love and self-control."

taunted to prove Himself, teased to call down the radiant armies of heaven. Yet He didn't—though He could have with a word. He was not concerned about justifying Himself or saving His reputation; instead, His merciful purpose was aimed at saving the lost and justifying humanity.

Rather than using His power for Himself, He used His power by *restraining* His power. At unspeakable cost, Jesus stewarded His untold power for the good of those who were crucifying Him. In love's humble service, He compassionately gave Himself to save His enemies. The gentle and lowly one was violently lifted up on the cross—splintered, pierced, and bleeding over the symbol of Rome's misuse of power. The cross, like a terrible mirror, was reflecting to the world its grotesque use of power, and like a window into heaven, it was granting a view into the heart of the self-sacrificing love of an all-powerful God. Split open like a seed, here is the God who reconciles a fragmented world.

The gentleness of God is the staggering power by which all things hold together.

13

Faithful Witness

Telling the Good News of Jesus with Words and Deeds

As kingfishers catch fire, dragonflies draw flame;
As tumbled over rim in roundy wells
Stones ring; like each tucked string tells, each hung bell's
Bow swung finds tongue to fling out broad its name;
Each mortal thing does one thing and the same:
Deals out that being indoors each one dwells;
Selves—goes itself; *myself* it speaks and spells,
Crying *What I do is me: for that I came.*
　　—Gerard Manley Hopkins, "As Kingfishers Catch Fire"

In its profundity I saw—ingathered and bound by love
into one single volume—what, in the universe seems
separate, scattered.

　　　　　　　　　　　　　—Dante, *Paradiso*

I carry the conversation with me, like a peculiar scar that
makes you smile when you remember how you came by it. I
was sitting in his study, still wearing my uncomfortable
work shirt with its literal blue collar. It was a Friday afternoon, and I had just finished the last service call of the day.
And like the other Fridays of recent months, I had clocked

out and made my way to the church, had a short conversation with the ever-kind Margie at the reception desk, and then went about scouring the metal shelves of the small church library for something, for anything in a cover or title that would catch light and call me to it. I was not looking for a mere book. I was excavating for a treasure I had heard rumors of. At some point in my hunting for authors and ideas and words to minister to my soul, he would walk into the room of musty books and say my name with mirth and warmth. I never doubted that he delighted in my presence. But I would be lying if I said it wasn't an impassable mystery to me.

And just like every other Friday, we would walk into his humble study, sit down in well-worn chairs, and talk for a good while. Pastor Tom had not only been my wife's pastor for as long as she could remember, but he was also the father of her best friend. Which means my wife had witnessed him at home playing games and making mac and cheese for the kids, being the chauffeur in the loud minivan on various outings, as well as in the pulpit preaching. He was now my pastor as well. And over time, I, too, had seen the alluring absence of self-consciousness, of childlike wonder and coherence between the pulpit and his way of life.

Over the months of our deepening friendship, there seemed to be a converging of two great circles God had drawn in my life, like some real-life Venn diagram of overlapping worlds: the plumbing truck and the pastor's study; my father the master plumber and my friend the pastor. Over the months, Pastor Tom and I had conversations that helped map my soul. We talked about Scripture, current events, our families, my issues, the melancholic poems I had been writing. Our conversations took us on winding walks through the writings of Fyodor Dostoevsky to Dorothy Sayers, Dietrich Bonhoeffer to Flannery O'Connor, Herman Melville to Abraham Heschel. At times he would have me join him at weddings and funerals, uncomfortable hospital visits and lively theology classes—all that I might watch and see and then discuss with him. He was shepherding me in the ways of shepherding. He had invited me into his way of life. *Come and see.* It was an unexpected apprenticeship.

On that Friday, sitting there in both physical and existential discomfort in my blue collar, I was grumbling about my lot in life and how I felt like I was crawling my way through wasted days. Pastor Tom listened for a bit and then leaned in. He looked at me with the usual kindness and conviction his bright eyes held, and he told me in very clear terms: "Your grumbling is unhealthy, unhelpful, and unholy." And then, with just as much gravity as brightness, he said, "I believe that at some point you will look back on these days and thank God for them, for the gift they are that you just can't see yet. Through them He is changing you into who you really are." There was no divine illumination in that moment. My response was a cynical "yeah, right" sort of thing. I faked a half smile to stay polite and hide in my not-okay-ness. I could not see.

But he was right. I am thankful for those days of cobwebbed crawl spaces and broken pipes as I learned the unexpected rhythms of apprenticeship. And I am thankful for those days of shepherding from him, who, like a pastoral Yoda, was humbly showing me the way of Jesus in the everydayness of it all. Pastor Tom was a faithful witness to me—the audio and video of his life were uncommonly in sync.

HOLDING IT TOGETHER

Have you ever tried to watch an online video with a bad connection—the visuals glitching and the audio detached, floating irritatingly out of sync? Or maybe you've seen a badly dubbed kung fu movie from the seventies? If so, you have experienced the unpleasant feeling of cognitive dissonance—a mismatch between expectations and experience. It's not just annoying, it is mentally distressing as the brain has to work overtime to integrate the disparate signals. What should be a coherent whole is experienced as conflicting pieces.

In our cultural moment, we have seen the rise of a controlling virtue that can be called "authenticity of being." This ache for authenticity is an expression of our longing to experience something whole and coherent in a world of fragments and masks. A desire for something true from skin to core in a world of fallen leaders, catfish filters, and curated images. At its root, it is an ache for God.

Jesus is the perfectly integrated, fully in sync, utterly congruent human being. He is authenticity incarnate. There is no dissonance in His being, no shadow, no disjointedness, no distance between the *ought* and *is* of His life. And so, apprentices of Jesus are those who are becoming more and more congruent, more coherent, as they become like Him. But sadly, there is a great deal more glitching pixels and disorienting out-of-sync audio/video in the church than we are comfortable admitting. We need to grow in Christlikeness through the practice of faithful witness:

Faithful witness is telling the good news of Jesus with words and deeds.

In Matthew's gospel, just before the Sermon on the Mount, we read about the deeply integrated audio/video of Jesus's life of faithful witness. Matthew 4v23–24 tells us:

> He went throughout all Galilee, teaching in their synagogues and proclaiming the gospel of the kingdom and healing every disease and every affliction among the people. So his fame spread throughout all Syria, and they brought him all the sick, those afflicted with various diseases and pains, those oppressed by demons, those having seizures, and paralytics, and he healed them.

His audio is loud and clear: He is teaching about the kingdom of God, preaching that true life has come near, that a with-God life has opened up in our midst and is accessible to all. His video is synced with His words: He is healing every disease, showing love and care to all who are afflicted. This man is magnetic. The crowds, like charged iron filings, fly toward Him in their hopes and hurts. He is no mere puff of air, no orator of empty words. He is not untethered action—He speaks words of life and light while His actions undo the darkness. He has breath from heaven in His lungs and Earth's iron in His warm blood.

Let's go to Capernaum for a moment to witness this. The text is found in Mark 2v1–12.

Capernaum is a small fishing village on the north shore of the Sea of Galilee. For some three years it was where Jesus lived and had His home base for ministry. As we step into the story here, Jesus has been out on the road touring, doing marvelous works. He has been saying beautiful things, reshaping the imaginations of an oppressed people with kingdom wisdom. He has been touching the untouchable and healing the things thought unhealable. And now, when He comes home to this humble fishing village, the crowds close in like moths to a lantern.

In these verses, we find Jesus preaching to a full house—literally. He is in a modest home swollen with people, the crowd spilling out of windows and clustered at the door. It is a crush of hope. No room to move. No one can get in. The fire marshal would have shut this party down if he were on the scene. Why the clamor and crowding? Word and deed. Jesus has been gospeling the neighborhood with kingdom words and kingly works. He has left a wake of the un-possessed, the un-blinded, the now clean, and the once-leprous. He is a one-of-a-kind rabbi and wonderworker.

Back on home turf, He is preaching again, and the people are hanging on to His words for dear life:

> When he returned to Capernaum after some days, it was reported that he was at home. And many were gathered together, so that there was no more room, not even at the door. And he was preaching the word to them.[1]

---

1 Mark 2v1–2.

He is preaching *the word* to them. The word of the kingdom. That is, He is proclaiming the good news that the long-awaited God-promised renewal of all things has arrived in Him, and that now it can be "on earth as it is in heaven" because God's will is being done in Jesus. Then the roof comes off.

> They came, bringing to him a paralytic carried by four men. And when they could not get near him because of the crowd, they removed the roof above him, and when they had made an opening, they let down the bed on which the paralytic lay.[2]

So taken by the congruent words and deeds of Jesus, friends of a paralyzed man don't let a problem of maximum occupancy stop them. They scramble to the housetop, make a new sunroof, and lower their friend into the presence of Jesus. And Jesus, who I imagine as grinning while dusting roof debris from His shoulders, watches in wonder. He then tells the paralytic to get up and jog home. Well, not quite yet. First, He aims His love at the man's inner depths.

> When Jesus saw their faith, he said to the paralytic, "Son, your sins are forgiven." Now some of the scribes were sitting there, questioning in their hearts, "Why does this man speak like that? He is blaspheming! Who can forgive sins but God alone?"[3]

---

2 Mark 2v3–4.
3 Mark 2v5–7.

Unexpectedly, Jesus says, "Son, your sins are forgiven." The air is now charged with crackling electricity. All were expecting Jesus to heal lifeless legs, not reshape a man's soul. They anticipated a "Get on up, son. Time to dance!" not a forgiveness of sins. To the gasps of the religious leaders in attendance, Jesus delivers the good news of the kingdom to a man who can't yet dance. Jesus, the great physician, goes after what is really killing the man—the dis-integrating force of sin within him. What this man needs is the deeper healing of a sin-atrophied soul. But are these empty words that any unstable Nazarene might say in delusions of grandeur? Any madman can say "forgiven."

> Immediately Jesus, perceiving in his spirit that they thus questioned within themselves, said to them, "Why do you question these things in your hearts? Which is easier, to say to the paralytic, 'Your sins are forgiven,' or to say, 'Rise, take up your bed and walk'?"[4]

Jesus knows doubt about His words is rioting in their hearts—*How dare this Jesus from Nowhereville claim to do what only the God of heaven can do! And easy to say, that word forgiveness! It can't be proven. Charlatan. Look, the poor man still lies there on his dirty mat!*

Jesus then shows in ultra-high fidelity the perfectly synced audio/video of the kingdom of God that is available through Him.

> "That you may know that the Son of Man has authority on earth to forgive sins"—he said to the paralytic—"I say to

---

4 Mark 2v8–9.

you, rise, pick up your bed, and go home." And he rose and immediately picked up his bed and went out before them all, so that they were all amazed and glorified God, saying, "We never saw anything like this!"[5]

"That you may know," He says. In other words, "Let the goodness of my deed reveal the truth of my words." And the man's long-dead legs come buzzing and shaking to life. But more so, an inner vitality rises from the dust and begins to dance. His sins have been forgiven by his creator and redeemer. This man's long exile from a with-God life is over. Jesus has just witnessed in both word and deed to the Father's love and goodness. The people are wonderstruck. Rightfully so.

IF NECESSARY?

You might have heard it before. It is an increasingly popular quote: "Preach the gospel at all times. Use words if necessary." It is attributed to Saint Francis of Assisi, and it has a subversive and savvy feel to it. The problem is, Francis never said it. Not even close. Yes, Francis was a man of action, disavowing his robust trust fund, giving away his Air Jordans and G-Wagon, and embracing a life of simplicity and solitude. And, yes, he served the poor and was a voice for the voiceless. But he was also an avid preacher of the gospel. Even preaching to the animals, so the stories say. He taught that our practices must match our preaching, not replace it.[6]

---

5 Mark 2v10–12.

6 The closest Francis seems to have come to saying something that resembles this misattributed quote is found in his *Rule of 1221*, which speaks to how one

The gospel needs words. The word *gospel* comes from the Greek word *euangelion*. The *eu* bit means "good." Think of words like *eulogy* (good word) or *euphoria* (good feeling). The *angelion* part means "message" or "news."[7] So *euangelion,* or *gospel* as we know it in English, is a telling, a sharing, a proclaiming of something good that has happened in history. It is not something that can be intuited. It cannot be discerned from the movement of the stars or a meadowlark's song. It must be told. Words are necessary in gospeling, and gospeling should be a regular practice for apprentices of Jesus.

The gospel is not merely a private message of personal salvation. It is a public and cosmic declaration that the kingdom of God is now open and available in Jesus Christ—a King whose administration of love is on the move reshaping the world and our hearts. The gospel is the good news that God has stepped into history in the person and work of Jesus Christ; that He has brought eternal life through His presence, faithfulness, and suffering; that He fulfilled the law and promises of God at just the right time in just the right way; that He did what we could not do while dis-integrated in our sin; that He died in our place to take upon Himself the death sin brings, to forgive us and cleanse us, to grant us the gift of a new God-united nature, and to pour into our hearts His Spirit to empower us. He came to call us into partnership with Him in the re-gardening of this world for total, mutual, eternal flourishing in His presence to the praise of His glory.

---

should practice their preaching with integrity by way of the life they live: "No brother should preach contrary to the form and regulations of the holy Church nor unless he has been permitted by his minister. . . . All the Friars . . . should preach by their deeds."

7 Strong's Greek Lexicon, "euangelion," Blue Letter Bible, www.blueletter bible.org/lexicon/g2098/kjv/tr/0-1.

That kind of good news is far better than some banal go-to-heaven-when-you-die benefits card for our spiritual back pockets. It is a multidimensional, multifaceted, multivalent treasure from the bright heart of heaven that is at work renewing the present world. And this is news that must be told. It is not self-evident when you bring your sick neighbor a warm meal. Sure, they need the meal. But more than that, they need the life-giving love of Jesus to nourish their souls. Give them both.

This is why Romans 10v13–17 tells us:

"Everyone who calls on the name of the Lord will be saved." *How then will they call on him* in whom they have not believed? And how are they to believe in him of whom they have never heard? And how are they to hear without someone preaching? And how are they to preach unless they are sent? As it is written, "How beautiful are the feet of those who preach the good news!" But they have not all obeyed the gospel. For Isaiah says, "Lord, who has believed what he has heard from us?" So faith comes from hearing, and hearing through the word of Christ.

And then there are Jesus's words in Acts 1v8:

You will receive power when the Holy Spirit has come upon you, and you will be my witnesses in Jerusalem and in all Judea and Samaria, and to the end of the earth.

Jesus's apprentices are to be witnesses. To be a witness is not just to see something and then move on. It is not to be a spectator or voyeur. It is to tell others what you have seen, now know, or have experienced firsthand. We are to witness about this Jesus we have met, telling others the good news of who He is and what He has done. It's simply impossible to preach the gospel without words. Yet reductive tendencies have us thinking in ungodly *either/or* ways rather than divine *both/and* ways. The commonplace severing of words and deeds has brought harm to the church, sending collateral damage tearing through communities in which we live. Movements of benevolent action that meet physical needs but never show how the rays of light can be traced back to Jesus can leave confusion about what love is and isn't. Kind gestures never linked to good news often leave people stuck in their darkness clinging to terrible gods. Dots never connected and lines never drawn leave needed portraits of Jesus unpainted.

On the other hand, charismatic teachers and pulpiteers ply impressive skill and rhetorical principles while exhorting us to follow Jesus, but offstage their bullish ways blur the message. An eighty-year-old congregant who has never missed a Sunday in half a century can quote Scripture with ease but is flat-out mean and is the CGO (chief grumbling officer) of the community. His daughter wants nothing to do with him or the hypocrisy of the church after all these years. Then there is that co-worker who backbites his boss and cheats his way through projects, but keeps quoting Romans 8 and inviting you to church. There are many ways we can sever words and deeds, becoming unfaithful witnesses.

ON YOUR TONGUE AND TEETH

So how do we practice being faithful witnesses? First—and the reason this practice is listed last among the seven—is that we practice the other six practices. We embody the way of Jesus through the other exercises that translate into myriad kingdom deeds. Alongside such practices, we speak forth the beauty, the goodness, and the truth of the gospel.

We learn to verbalize it. To taste the truth on our tongue and teeth. We should be practicing saying aloud and explaining the gospel of Jesus. It's interesting how we might rehearse a marriage proposal dozens of times before kneeling with the ring, or obsessively prepare for a pivotal presentation for work, yet we can think it silly or inauthentic to practice telling the good news. Given the gospel's grandeur, it would be helpful and healthy for us to be able to talk about it in both short and long forms. Being able to do so will cultivate a habit of meditating on and preaching the gospel to yourself, and it will be helpful in sharing the gospel in different circumstances.

Here is a simple and pregnant way to articulate the gospel:

Jesus is Lord.

These three ancient words are like a drop of blood that holds a whole body of DNA swirling within. They are a small seed with a sprawling vineyard coiled inside. We should learn to see them as a spring-loaded shorthand for Jesus as the good King who rules and reigns over everything. They are a compressed version of Colossians 1v16–20:

By him all things were created, in heaven and on earth, visible and invisible, whether thrones or dominions or rulers or authorities—all things were created through him and for him. And he is before all things, and in him all things hold together. And he is the head of the body, the church. He is the beginning, the firstborn from the dead, that in everything he might be preeminent. For in him all the fullness of God was pleased to dwell, and through him to reconcile to himself all things, whether on earth or in heaven, making peace by the blood of his cross.

Jesus is Lord. Three potent and easy words to memorize and share. And then, each word can be opened up, reveled in.

Jesus: The name of a real, historic human being, a Jewish man from Nazareth who is humanity's Savior. His name, *Yeshua,* means *God is salvation.* This God-man has come near and made His kingdom available to us through His life, death, resurrection, and ascension. Through His sacrificial love we are saved by grace. Grace is God's benevolent action on our behalf. It is the goodness of God doing for us what we could not do ourselves. Jesus, then, is the greatest instance of grace. He is the goodness of God.

Is: Not *was,* not someday *will be.* But *is.* Now. Presently. Jesus did something in history that is now and forever in effect. He rules and reigns both now and eternally. We are His people in this present moment, and we will forever be His people, dwelling with Him in the new creation.

Lord: He is King. He has utter authority over life and death; He has sovereign power to rule and reign and redeem the farthest reaches of a fragmented world. Caesar is not the Lord who brings salvation. Neither is any manifestation of power, pleasure, riches, or anything else in creation. Only

Jesus can save and satisfy those made in His image. To be the people of the King and kingdom is to love and give allegiance to Him who loves and faithfully cares for us.

Now, here is a longer form that weaves the pieces together and has helped me share the three-dimensional beauty of the gospel:

The gospel is the good news of God the Father's loving, redemptive, and dramatic intervention in our sin-fractured world through the person and work of Jesus Christ and the empowering presence of His Spirit—to create for Himself a people of love and joy, who will partner with Him in re-gardening the world and dwell with Him forever, for God's glory and humanity's flourishing.

Rehearse these things. Talk to yourself about them. Get these words on your lips and into the muscle memory of your tongue. Practice saying them and explaining them—gladly putting the pieces together to help others re-imagine the world in which they live.

TELL YOUR STORY OF GRACE

Think about this for a moment: What do you, without doing any research, without any study or memorization work, without help from some app or AI, know so well that you can talk about it at a moment's notice? *You.*

This is what you know best—your story, your life. Now, admittedly, we all need to do the work of connecting the dots of our lives, mapping the terrain of our family of origin, becoming aware of who and what has formed us. That said, for those who are apprentices of Jesus, those who have shema-ed His call to "come and see," who have begun walking the trail and have the Master's dust on them, there is a story of transformation to share. There is an "I once was" and an "I now am" tale to tell. We each have a two-part story of how the grace of God has brought renewal. We all, in our own words, can say what John Newton, a human trafficker turned pastor, once said,

> I am not what I ought to be! . . . I am not what I wish to be! . . . I am not what I hope to be! . . . Yet, though I am not what I ought to be, . . . I am not what I once was—a slave to sin and Satan; and I can heartily join with the Apostle, and acknowledge; *By the grace of God, I am what I am!*[8]

I encourage you to devote some time to understanding your own history, connecting the dots of your experience, exploring the unmapped regions of your life story. Take a walk and pray for the Lord to lead you in these explorations, to search you and let you know what He sees. Sit with a friend, a spouse, or a counselor, and explore the narrative of your life. Learn to articulate what it is that has happened.

Apprentices of Jesus are a people who have His name on their lips, ready to gladly tell the story of who we once were and who we now are on this road of becoming like Him. And

---

8 "Anecdote of the Late Rev. John Newton," *The Christian Spectator* 3, no. 4 (1821): 186, www.google.com/books/edition/The_Christian_Spectator/mv4o AAAAYAAJ?q=ah.

here is one of the wonderful things about this commission of faithful witnessing, which we see in Matthew 28v18–20:

> Jesus came and said to them, "All authority in heaven and on earth has been given to me. Go therefore and make disciples of all nations, baptizing them in the name of the Father and of the Son and of the Holy Spirit, teaching them to observe all that I have commanded you. And behold, I am with you always, to the end of the age."

This is what is often called the Great Commission, and it comes with a great promise. In it is the call for all apprentices of Jesus to be witnesses in word and deed, in explicit gospel proclamation and teaching. Jesus is inviting us to be *tellers* of the best of all possible messages, and more so, He is assuring us He will always be with us, empowering us to do so. He promises we won't go witnessing alone. There is no need to fear failure or be anxious about it. He is with us, united to us, His grace covering our missteps, His love working good through our stumbles.

How is the practice of faithful witness possible for a stumbling and in-process people like us? Through His empowering presence. Remember, *union* precedes and upholds all our practices of *abiding* and *obeying*.

NECESSARILY CRUCIFORM

One last painful bit on this: There is no faithful witness without sacrifice. There is no apprenticeship to Jesus without a cross. One of the most profound ways to practice faithful witness is to suffer well—to grieve with hope. Suffering comes to us all. No one gets out of this life unscathed. Mortal blows and sacred wounds are everywhere. But for many, the suffering is squandered. Most of us work tenaciously to avoid this suffering—swerving around it, stuffing it, numbing it, pretending it isn't there. But the way of Jesus and therefore the way of apprenticeship is a cruciform way. It is the way of rejoicing and lamenting.

We know what God's will for us is no matter what comes our way. First Thessalonians 5v16–18 makes it clear: "Rejoice always, pray without ceasing, give thanks in all circumstances; for this is the will of God in Christ Jesus for you." And in Paul's letter to the Philippians, which was written from the moldering confines of prison, Paul writes, "Rejoice in the Lord always; again I will say, rejoice."[9] And then there is James, the brother of Jesus, who has the nerve and love to tell us:

> Count it all joy, my brothers, when you meet trials of various kinds, for you know that the testing of your faith produces steadfastness. And let steadfastness have its full effect, that you may be perfect and complete, lacking in nothing.[10]

Let me be clear: The rejoicing amid suffering that is a faithful witness is not a plastic, schmaltzy rejoicing. It is authentic rejoicing that doesn't minimize suffering or bypass heartache. A rejoicing that comes from an integrated soul that knows joy and suffering are not mutually exclusive but can

---

9 Philippians 4v4.
10 James 1v2–4.

coexist in the same heart, like rain glowing in the sunlight of a summer storm.

Faithfulness requires lament. So, a few words on the misunderstood gift of lament—a near-forgotten practice among the Western church. Lament is not simply walking through the stages of grief or crying out in pain. There is an *other*-aimed orientation to lament, as it is a form of prayer. "Laments are prayers that erupt from wounds," writes Kathleen O'Connor.[11] "Lament is a prayer in pain that leads to trust. . . . Think of lament as the transition between pain and promise," writes Mark Vroegop.[12] Lament is not faithlessness or complaining. It is faithfulness in the furnace. It is a holy protesting, a pushing back against what has collapsed in a world that was designed for shalom. It is not resignation, but a wrestling to cling to a God who says, "It is good."

When one spends time meditating on the book of Psalms and the book of Lamentations, a pattern emerges regarding the way of lament. It looks like this:

The Address → The Ache → The Ask → The Ascent

The *address* is simply turning to God in prayer. The God of the Scriptures is addressed as our hope and our wounded healer. He is to be trusted with the rawness of our soul and the darkness of the situation. The *ache* is the honest pouring out of the pain, giving voice to the suffering, entering into it, refusing to medicate it with some unreality. The *ask* is the peti-

---

11 Kathleen O'Connor, *Lamentations and the Tears of the World* (Orbis, 2002), 9.

12 Mark Vroegop, *Dark Clouds, Deep Mercy: Discovering the Grace of Lament* (Crossway, 2019), 28.

tion for God to act, to enter into the brokenness and do something according to His promises. It is to treat Him as God, as the one who can bind up the brokenhearted, the one who can give us beauty for our smoldering ash heaps. The *ascent* is a renewal of trust in God, a galvanized assurance that God is faithful and will keep His covenant with His people. It is a fortified hope rising from the embers. A rebirth from the death that kindled the lament. It is a greater glory born through the agony.

The practice of lament, in its refusal to minimize the pain while ruthlessly clinging to hope for renewal, is a profound witness to a watching world. There is something about actions of unrelenting love amid suffering that cut through the fog of arguments and opinions, that give otherworldly weight to our words, that grant gravity to our faith. It is when faithful witness slams face-first into concrete suffering that people utter things like, "How is it you have any joy left in your life—after all you have been through? How has grief not capsized your soul? How can you have such calm in the wake of your diagnosis?" As apprentices of Jesus, we are to follow His way of facing suffering: with an unflinching realism of the pain and an uncanny trust in the Father.

The goodness of God is not measured by convenience and comfort, but by the cross of Jesus Christ.

BRIGHT STARS AND TONS OF BRONZE

I am reminded of two things: bright stars and a ton of bronze. There is a parable by Danish philosopher, poet, and theologian Søren Kierkegaard that says,

When the prosperous man on a dark but starlit night drives comfortably in his carriage and has the lanterns lighted, aye, then he is safe, he fears no difficulty, he carries his light with him, and it is not dark close around him; but precisely because he has the lanterns lighted, and has a strong light close to him, precisely for this reason he cannot see the stars. For his lights obscure the stars, which the poor peasant driving without lights can see gloriously in the dark but starry night.[13]

In this world there are some splendors we can see only in the dark. There are some needful praises born only from the contractions of a sorrow-shaken soul.

There is no apprenticeship to a crucified Master that is without cruciformity. In His goodness, He will snuff out lanterns and lead us into dark but starry nights. There is no cross-less life of walking with Jesus. There is no new life without an old death.

To come full circle to the congruent words and deeds of Jesus, we go from a parable in Copenhagen back to the ruins of Capernaum, Jesus's seaside ministry home base. Remember, it was here that Jesus preached the good news to a full house, where the roof was torn off the party and He healed a paralyzed man after getting to the heart of the issue.

The first time I visited the village of Capernaum, I saw a homeless person sleeping on a park bench up ahead of us. As we approached the bench on our way to the synagogue ruins, I realized the homeless man was not alive. He was made of bronze. So curious—this life-size statue of a homeless man,

---

13 Søren Kierkegaard, *The Gospel of Suffering and the Lilies of the Field*, trans. David Swenson and Lillian Swenson (Augsburg, 1948), 123.

obscured under a cloak and asleep on a common park bench. This statue brazenly stood out from so many of the other pieces of art and ancient artifacts we had seen in the Holy Land. I stopped to look at it for a moment, wondering, *Why this, why here?* And then the penny dropped, and my emotions spiked.

This sculpted cloaked figure, which could have been any man, wasn't—because there, split wide in the top of the bronze bare feet, were the crucifixion's nail wounds. This was Jesus. I was upended.

This statue is simply called *Homeless Jesus* and is the brilliant work of artist Timothy Schmalz. Every time I walk by the provocative work, a visceral reaction calls me to contemplate the massive mystery the fifteen hundred pounds of bronze confront me with—the immensity of divine love in the flesh. To see Jesus so radically identified with humanity that I quickly assumed Him to be a homeless man and reflexively mapped a blanket of snap judgments and opinions over Him—it broke through my film of familiarity, opened my eyes wider to the wonder and the scandal of the kingdom.

On that park bench was a subtle-turned-startling portrayal of the One whose words harmonized with His deeds. Whose talk of love for the brokenhearted was wholly matched by His meeting them in their cosmic homelessness and places of pain. His words of divine love mirrored His sacred wounds. Wounds shaped like mouths, speaking healing. Jesus is the King of startling congruency.

This Jesus, this faithful witness to His Father's love, has made us His apprentices so that His divine love might be found in us, bodied forth in our lives. That we too might enter the places of pain as agents of healing love. He has come to make us "partakers of the divine nature."[14] He has opened the kingdom of God here in our midst, in our neighborhoods, making it possible to abide with Him, obey Him, and, degree by degree, become more like Him.

We can change. Come and see.

AT THE CLOSE AND THE CONTINUING ON

We have come to the close. You will read this a good deal after the fact, but today is the autumnal equinox—Sunday, September 22, 2024. It is also the day I gather up these months of writing and send these pages to my patient editor. This means, just like at the start, it is the fall. Again, I am hearing the haunting songs of geese as they navigate the bright September sky in wise formation. The ordered earth moves. Migration patterns mark time. Known rhythms usher us to new ways of being. Repetitions bring revelations. And it strikes me, in the crooning of their familiar southerly songs, they sound somehow different after all these years. I am no longer who I was those two decades ago when the locust trees were catching the season's fire, and I was skulking about in that alley of broken things. Though, I am still a man in process—somewhere midway through my great undragoning.

Jesus has brought about a bright and great quiet that has been growing inside the old clamor within. He has brought about a growing with-God-ness since that day I saw a glimpse of delight in that fire-made mirror. I have looked upon the smiling face of my heavenly Father for some time now. I have

---

14 2 Peter 1v4.

looked upon His goodness in the land of the living—in the sound of children running through the house in play, in disinfected hospital rooms and labored last words. I have looked upon His goodness at gravesides and wedding altars, and in an unexpected life of shepherding a people. I have looked upon His goodness in quiet places, and heard it in the ringing laughter of friends around dining room tables. All things, in some way or another, seem charged with God's grandeur. His delight has changed me.

I was in an alley behind a crumbling, boarded-up home with broken pipes in my hand when my imagination was baptized. I don't know where you are on your life's journey, but wherever this finds you, I pray the pieces of this book would come together and catch some heavenly slant of light, that you would see a glimpse of a smiling Father's love for you. May some glimmering of His divine delight meet you where you are. I trust that, even now, He is about His unhurried work of de-fragmenting you, re-forming you, inviting you further into the wholeness of who you are to be.

Take heart, He is on the move making wrecked things new and healing wonderblind eyes. Jesus, the "luminary Nazarene," as Einstein once called Him, "is before all things, and in him all things hold together."[15] And so, whatever may come our way, "all shall be well; and all manner of thing shall be well."[16] No matter what befalls those who are united to this blue-collar King, "what will survive of us is love."[17]

---

15 Colossians 1v17.

16 The words of Julian of Norwich, quoted from John Skinner, *Julian of Norwich: A Revelation of Love* (Gracewing, 2004), 47.

17 Philip Larkin, *Collected Poems,* ed. and with introduction by A. Thwaite (Farrar, Straus and Giroux, 1989), 110–11.

May His face shine upon you as you learn to walk with Him.

> Now may the God of peace himself sanctify you completely, and may your whole spirit and soul and body be kept blameless at the coming of our Lord Jesus Christ. He who calls you is faithful; he will surely do it.[18]

---

18 1 Thessalonians 5v23–24.

Acknowledgments

Madeleine L'Engle once spoke of writing as a form of prayer. Amen. There are many wonderful people who have helped me pray this book into being, and I thank you.

King Jesus, all the words in an infinite array of books could never fully attest to Your beauty, goodness, and truth. You are brilliant in every known and unexplored sense of the word. Your "love bade me welcome" and brought me into Your joy.

Marla Joy, I am still reaching for words to express my love for you. You walk in wisdom and are a luminous grace on this road home. In so many ways, this book would not exist without you. My kids—Haven, Silas, Hadley, Olivia, and Ruby—I love you to the moon and back. May you grow in wonder and valor and glad-heartedness. The Hardesty, Teebken, and Sloan families, thank you for your steadfast love and support.

Don Pape, for hearing unheard voices, for unyielding advocacy, and for your bright mirth. You are the Tom Bombadil of literary agents. Jay Kim, for your sharp mind and humble heart—and for asking if I had a book in me. Jon Tyson, for the glowing embers, kindred conversations, and simply sharing in the glorious wonder of it all. John Mark Comer, your uncommon kindness has been a gift. Thank you for exceptional food, unflagging encouragement, a timely "What! You too?" and a healing walk through the sage of the Santa Ana hills. Jefferson Bethke, for radical hospitality, ruthless pickle-balling, and wild drives on Sawtooth roads among other adventures.

Gerry Breshears, for pastoring pastors, taking my calls at all hours, and relentlessly asking, "What does the text say?" Western Seminary, for caring for the whole person and calling us into the light of community. Gabriel Webb, for fellowship in the deep things.

Kingfishers (Clay Worrell, Ryan Smith, Char Brodersen, Brad Witty, Daniel Huskey, and Adam Dobbs), your brotherhood opened its arms to me at just the right time. I miss our late Thursday nights and all-too-early Friday mornings. Mike Neglia, for sharing in a love of words and the Word. The Men's Council, for the journey so far, and to many more years of feasting and seeking out the hidden things.

Mark and Patti Lortz, for being there. Tom Hovestol, for showing the way and calling me "further up and further in." Leron Heath, for open hearts and open books beside early-morning fires.

Valley Community Church, it is a marvel that our Lord has granted me the gift of being one of your pastors all these years. To the congregation and entire leadership team, thank you for the winding roads walked, tears shed, laughter had, and wisdom shared in this life together. Dane Olney, for the way of repair and the fellowship of walking in the light. Bryan Hardwick, for brotherhood and the joy of co-laboring. A special thanks to the elders and ministry team for the care and encouragement to write these things.

Jake and Wildhouse Productions, for the laughter and photography. The team at Penguin Random House Christian, your belief in this book remains surreal. An immense thank you to Tina Constable, Laura Barker, Laura Wright, and Drew Dixon. Drew, thank you for seeing what this book could be and shepherding it along the way. Laura W., thank you for lending your keen eye and quick mind in the working of your copyediting magic.

HEATH HARDESTY serves as the lead pastor of Valley Community Church and is a founder of Inklings Coffee & Tea in the heart of downtown Pleasanton, California. Heath grew up in a blue-collar home and was a plumber's apprentice in Colorado before becoming a pastor on the edge of Silicon Valley where he and his family now reside. He holds degrees in literature, leadership, biblical studies, and theology from the University of Colorado Boulder and Western Seminary in Portland.

www.heathhardesty.com

@heathhardesty

About the Type

This book was set in Garamond, a typeface originally designed by the Parisian type cutter Claude Garamond (c. 1500–61). This version of Garamond was modeled on a 1592 specimen sheet from the Egenolff-Berner foundry, which was produced from types assumed to have been brought to Frankfurt by the punch cutter Jacques Sabon (c. 1520–80).

Claude Garamond's distinguished romans and italics first appeared in *Opera Ciceronis* in 1543–44. The Garamond types are clear, open, and elegant.